The Queering of an American Evangelical

The Queering of an American Evangelical

The Sermons, Statements, and Prayers of a Southern Baptist Minister

Rev. Jeff Hood

WIPF & STOCK · Eugene, Oregon

THE QUEERING OF AN AMERICAN EVANGELICAL
The Sermons, Statements, and Prayers of a Southern Baptist Minister

Wipf & Stock
An Imprint of Wipf and Stock Publishers
199 W. 8th Ave., Suite 3
Eugene, OR 97401

www.wipfandstock.com

PAPERBACK ISBN: 978-1-5326-1253-4
HARDCOVER ISBN: 978-1-5326-1255-8

Manufactured in the U.S.A. NOVEMBER 29, 2016

To George, who taught me to see.

To Emily, who taught me to love.

To Jeff and Phillip, who taught me to hope.

All Biblical Quotations that are not My Translation or Interpretation are Notated Before or After the Quote.
Some Passages are Notated Earlier in the Sermon with a Notation like this John 10-14 NASB…this Notation Indicates that all of the Passages that fit Within the Parameters Laid Out use the New American Standard Bible.

The Abbreviations for Each Version of the Bible are as Follows:

KJV: King James Version of the Bible
NASB: New American Standard Bible
NIV: New International Version of the Bible
NLT: New Living Translation of the Bible
NRSV: New Revised Standard Version of the Bible
RSV: Revised Standard Version of the Bible
The Message: The Message Version of the Bible

Foreword

It strikes common folk of the twenty-first century as odd that genuine transformation of an individual from a publicly espoused religious and moral perspective can and does occur. Many of us have become cynical about faith, and religion in particular, so inner spiritual transformation as such is suspect, if not just denied. We live inundated by the non-reality of public figures posing for attention, pretending their digitally captured lives are "real living." Such lives are recorded by camera crews, television producers, directors of sorts and—if as economically fortunate as the Kardashians—global corporate sponsorships. We have lost trust that "real" might continue to mean truth. That whatever is stated aloud might have a sliver of possibility of being heartfelt is humorous. Can a woman or a man of our present time be moved inwardly toward the more accepting and lovable end of a spectrum of religious practice or spiritual belief? We profoundly doubt it.

How would present-day people of faith treat a newly repentant, converted prosecutor and executioner of a select group of oppressed minorities? Let us propose that such a famous individual, one who has espoused moral authority in his (or her) cultural role of judge and punisher, were on afternoon talk cable television shows making the rounds. This person would now be attempting to influence the very people that he arrested or sent to their deaths. But this story has a twist: it sounds like our reformed villain had fallen off an old convertible after being struck by a miraculous light. Now during some interviews, we are convinced he has become an evangelist to the very people he was persecuting. We would wait for the commercial break, or some of us would, those who had not previously changed the channel to a competition reality program. This modern Paul (or Paula) would annoy many of us with this tale of borderline personality-shifting behavior.

> Now as he [Saul] was going along and approaching Damascus, suddenly a light from heaven flashed around him. He fell to the ground and heard a voice saying to him, "Saul, Saul, why do you persecute me?" He asked, "Who are you, Lord?" The reply came, "I am Jesus, whom you are persecuting. But get up and enter the city and you will be told what to do." (Acts 9:3-6, New Revised Standard Version)[1]

We have an opportunity offered by my colleague and spirit-filled brother, Rev. Jeff Hood, to witness a life in transformation, reminiscent of the first century Saul who became Paul. The force of the universe caused the collision of Hood and me while he was a prideful, conservative Southern Baptist and I was an African American seminarian married to my life partner of over fifteen years—another man. I was *out* at our diverse seminary, also as a Unitarian Universalist to top it all off. Reading this book, you will see through Hood's own Southern Baptist sermons an intimate and spiritual alteration transpire in the theology and the heart of my friend.

Do I believe this kind of change or not? Do I trust that someone who once told me directly in an auditorium filled with witnesses—predominately of liberal varieties of

[1] Acts 9:3-6, The first depiction of the conversion of Saul the Persecutor to Paul the Apostolic founder of the gentile Christian faith in *Acts of the Apostles*.

Christianity—that "homosexuality could not be the best that God has intended for his children"? I was stunned at the time by his conviction. I was intrigued more by the smile on his face, as though he knew he would have to love, carefully, all the homosexuals who were within the sound of his voice. This included me, the seasoned Black, gay activist seated across from him. Hood had to deliver "The Word," as he felt his sacred obligation to do so in that moment as much as Saul of Tarsus had in the first century.

The Queering of an American Evangelical is the result of his personal developments in the aftermath of this incident. Yes, in that lecture hall I had a response to Hood's proclamation about homosexuality. It was as if the universe were determined that Hood and I not only meet and conflict with each other, but that we discover that if brotherly love is expressed truthfully, it is all-powerful. Maybe love could be in the lives of the faithful who were seated in opposition to each other regarding homosexuality, gay liberation, and all things *Queer*. Maybe metamorphorphsis is not just necessary for caterpillars and dragonflies, but everyday hardheaded liberals and conservatives.

Can love change hearts? Do we have a choice about believing in this possibility of transformation as humans in this century? If we do not, do we have any alternative for surviving our own human interference with the whole of creation on the planet? Could love change my own activist-trained, more-than-middle-aged visions to include a conservative who spoke bigotry to my face? Not only my liberal friends, and the young, fellow leftists would I have to love. But to love everyone was the commandment, even a thinner, conservative, brilliant young man like Hood, who was in the throes of discovering what was vital to his life and his ministry. Could I love him? Could I even stomach having lunch with him? My curiosity was spirit-possessed and I desired to know more of his story. How did Hood come to be so calmly convinced of a hateful religious position and how could he smile with such care at the same time? If Hood truly believed my innate sexuality was an aberration of what God wanted, what He "truly" wanted for me, then why the sincere smile?

The story within this book is not one of a great fall by Hood, at least not from my observation deck. It is a story of a movement from one clearly held position to another of accepting a radical conclusion that has disrupted and recreated his entire ministry and existence. Hood and I saw past our being right, our blatant differences, and began a dialogue which has served us both through several difficult life transitions. He has faced his religious tradition, his family, and his friends with the ministry that now liberates and celebrates those he once sought to save from their homosexuality back in our seminary days. Our dependable friendship was one of the influences that, despite our beginning, helped Hood reform his previously held position. What do we believe about the transformation that must be accessible through relationships, an avenue through which love travels to alter our being?

We can try to preserve some sense that the world is not changing ever faster—faster than we want—while sitting and observing Hood's change unfolding, but not for long. The world is in the midst of transformations. These global shifts will best be served by a conscious people of faith and people of wonder. Change occurs rarely without pain, as the reader will hear Hood proclaim in this book. Our recognition of this common necessity, change and pain, not only for ourselves but for every element of the physical world, will help with the acceptance of Hood's changes and our own. The deafening, speeding pace of some growth and shedding of the old creates friction with strongly relied-upon aspects of our existence. This friction is a source of sparks, whether we consider them divine or just natural phenomena, sparks that light up our world.

The cell phone, for example, has revolutionized the capabilities of the most oppressed folks on the planet organizing to respond to whatever terror or dictator they are saddled with. The public acceptance of even something as benign and treacherous as same-sex marriage, another example, has risen to the point of assuredness of eventuality in our country. It is only a matter of time until some couples in various stages of queerness are—in the most creative style—destroying their unions on a new televised, Queer Divorce Court. The devoted viewers will laugh at the one-liners slipped to the various parties and executed with the ease of untrained entertainers.

Until then, let yourself pray, walk, and ride along with Hood to where he is assuredly called to be, following a queer savior. I am there also, but now as his friend, confidant, a chosen "uncle" to the Hood twins, and a devoted supporter of his saintly wife. Maybe reading Hood's book will begin a disturbance within you, a turmoil, or perhaps more slowly, an awakening of transformation.

Duncan E. Teague

Minister, Unitarian Universalist Association
Grand Marshall of Atlanta Pride 1993 and 2001
Namesake of the Duncan E. Teague Collection at the Auburn Avenue Research Library in Atlanta, Georgia, a collection focused on black and gay history
Profiled in *Sweet Tea* by E. Patrick Johnson[2]

---

[2] E. Patrick Johnson. "Sweet Tea: Black Gay Men of the South." Chapel Hill: University of North Carolina Press, 2008.

Preface

This is the story of someone who started out in Christian ministry as a sincere evangelical and became something else. This is my story. I share it through the acquired voice that either God gave or I choose...that of a Baptist preacher. Regardless of your persuasion, I have felt the presence of God. I think.

I am a cradle Southern Baptist. I grew up at the Rock Baptist Church...a church my forefathers and foremothers helped found over 125 years ago. This was not uncommon in the region where I grew up. In the South all have and hold on to history. My parents raised me in the midst of the evangelical explosion of the 1980s and 1990s. We were always seeking to work out our salvation with fear and trembling. We were always saving America. We were always desperately trying to save our own souls. Our pastor was an evangelical superstar of the local sort. He consistently begged us to ask the Lord to reside in our hearts. I did...oh I did.

For most of my high school years, I was a bruiser for God. I told everyone I suspected might be going to hell that they were indeed going to hell. I figured it was better to be safe than sorry. The truth was that I was fearful for my own soul. I was never quite sure. I acted out of that fear and wanted to get everyone saved. I figured if I saved all the people I knew and prayed enough there was no way God could keep me out of the pearly gates. This is not the best way to start out a life of ministry. The first sermon in this text is an example of the fruits of fear...

In college at Auburn University in Auburn, Alabama, I felt something. God whispered and I answered. While working at Wadley Baptist Church, I became a Southern Baptist preacher then an ordained Southern Baptist minister. I preached harder and harder. It felt like I was the voice of God. Ultimately, I found the Cloverdale Baptist Church. I worked with those the Bible calls the least. I found Jesus...perhaps for the first time undisguised. I felt a deeper call to ministry. I decided to go all the way. The Southern Baptist Theological Seminary was going to give me the means to be the minister that God called me to be. I wanted to ask questions and I found certainty. It didn't go well. The questions have guided me ever since.

The revelation of my mentor George Stewart changed my life. I lost my faith. I regained my faith. I found something new. Jesus appeared. It seems that Jesus appears when new revelations of love come. I grew tired of the Southern Baptist Theological Seminary and finished quickly. Don Fulton helped me push past the certainties and to a more inclusive future. My first stop at the Fountain Anglican Church was a bust. Lies, secrets, and ethical lapses bubbled beneath the veneer of charismatic answers. Emory University's Candler School of Theology gave me the time to readjust personal questions of God and existential reality, while gaining insight into the broad amazingly diverse theological world constantly blossoming around me. I developed a deep love for mystery and the minute points of light piercing the darkness.

I met two dear friends, Duncan Teague and Lucas Johnson. I would say that they primarily and the rest of the Queer Community broadly have served as my salvation.

In the few years following Candler...I searched and found deeper existential and theological questions in the mystery, I pursued and obtained degrees from the University of Alabama and Creighton University, I married Emily and had two beautiful boys named Jeff and Phillip, and I did a short stint in a doctoral program in U.S. History at the University of Mississippi. In these years, I changed the most. By the time we arrived in Texas, I knew who I was. I was different.

I am now an activist who loves mystery and despises the blatant certainties of bigotry. I function as a minister with a mysterious prophetic voice for a Jesus that is love. I, like Jesus, refuse to be subject to or defined by the oppressive normative constructions of my society or church. I am queer. I thank Steven Sprinkle for this discovery deep within myself. I am slowly learning what it means to be a street scholar pastor activist. I still believe in the salvation experience...but it looks much different. There are less answers and more love here. I believe that God is restoring all things to right. I get to see it all the time. I tell the tale of the restoration of my soul through the sermons I have preached. These are not perfect words. These sermons, prayers, and letters perhaps only on occasion changed the hearers who heard them but most of all they changed me. These words are my story up until the founding of The Church at Mable Peabody's, a queer church in Denton, Texas. This is the journey of a sincere follower of Christ. This is the Queering of an American Evangelical...

1.

Though I am apologetic and embarrassed for ever even delivering this sermon, I think these words are helpful to illustrate my evangelical origins. I grew up in a culture that believed the Bible to be the inerrant infallible word of God. I learned very early on that the Bible could be an incredible tool of both love and oppression. I was a sincere seeker of Jesus. I felt closest to Jesus when I was fighting for the Bible. When asked to give a short talk at a youth bible study, I had no question what subject I was going to tackle with full force.

Is Homosexuality a Sin? Yes.

The Rock Baptist Church

Rex, Georgia

May 12, 2002

Pleasant evening. We believe in God...correct? We believe that Jesus is God's son...correct? How do we know anything about God? Do we make it up? Of course not... We know because God has revealed himself to us in the Bible. Without the Bible, we would not know anything. Does God make mistakes? No. Is God powerful enough to keep his word intact? Either he is powerful enough or he is not God. The Bible is the inerrant infallible word of God because God made it so. We can trust the Bible on all matters of life, faith, and practice. So when I was asked to prepare a short little talk...I chose the topic of homosexuality and turned to the Bible.

First, I looked at Genesis 1 and 2. God creates Adam a man and Eve a woman in his image and tells them to multiply. Does God create Adam and Steve? No. Does God create Andrea and Eve? No. God did not create any function that would allow men or women to multiply independent of the opposite sex. God did create functions by which males and females could multiply together. God told Adam and Eve to multiply. It was a command. To do anything else than seek to multiply is a sin. From the beginning of time, God created and blessed heterosexuality. God did not create and God has not blessed homosexuality. God created heterosexuality, which means that heterosexuality is of God and anything that diverges from heterosexuality is not of God.

Second, I looked to Genesis 19:1-29. Two male angels came to the city of Sodom and visited the home of Lot. The wicked men of the city wanted to have sex with the male angels and surrounded the house. God saved Lot and his family and then destroyed the city by raining fiery brimstone on it. God killed the homosexuals for their wicked behavior. This scripture clearly illustrates God taking action against a specific sexual orientation...homosexuality. These scriptures leave little doubt that homosexuals are ravenous and often desire to take advantage of all people...especially males. Like in Sodom, they will ascend on your house at night and seek to have sex with whatever men they find. The fact that the verses talk about all the men of the city, young and old, ascending on the house means that the older homosexuals taught the younger homosexuals how to be predators just like them. Homosexuality is a perversion that often leads to the perversion of children...which we call molestation. Sodom is the origin of the word sodomy...what homosexuals do when they are behind close doors. They exchange natural sexual relations for unnatural relations. Sodom provides clear evidence that God punishes homosexuals and anything that God punishes is by definition a sin.

Third, I studied two passages from Leviticus, 18:22 and 20:13 (NASB). First, Leviticus 18:22 states, "You shall not lie with a male as one lies with a female; it is an abomination." Abomination means something that is disgusting or revolting to God. Since we are reading God's word, then that means that God himself is saying that homosexuality is disgusting and revolting. How can we believe that anything that is called an abomination is not a sin? The answer is simple...we can't. Second, Leviticus 20:13 states, "If *there is* a man who lies with a male as those who lie with a woman, both of them have committed a detestable act; they shall surely be put to death. Their bloodguiltiness is upon them." Did you hear what God said? He says that homosexuality is so sinful that we should kill the homosexuals. We are showing so much grace right now by not reacting like God tells us to in the face of their parades and public kisses. It is hard for me not to believe that homosexuality is a sin when God tells us to kill those who perpetrate homosexual acts. There are so many who will argue that these type of passages are just in the Old Testament...well then, let's move to the New Testament.

Fourth, I spent time with Romans 1:24-27 (NASB), "Therefore God gave them over in the lusts of their hearts to impurity, so that their bodies would be dishonored among them. For they exchanged the truth of God for a lie, and worshiped and served the creature rather than the Creator, who is blessed forever. Amen. For this reason God gave them over to degrading passions; for their women exchanged the natural function for that which is unnatural, and in the same way also the men abandoned the natural function of the woman and burned in their desire toward one another, men with men committing indecent acts and receiving in their own persons the due penalty of their error." The Apostle Paul states that God gave people over to their homosexual desires as a punishment for their homosexual acts. The people thus sinned by thinking homosexual thoughts and committing homosexual acts...it is plain as day right here. A homosexual is completely outside of the will of God and therefore apart from God. God believes that homosexuality is a sin and God punishes the homosexual...unless there is total repentance I do not see anyway that a homosexual can be a Christian.

Fifth, I went to 1 Corinthians 6:9-10 (NASB), "Or do you not know that the unrighteous will not inherit the kingdom of God? Do not be deceived; neither fornicators, nor idolaters, nor adulterers, nor effeminate, nor homosexuals, nor thieves, nor *the* covetous, nor drunkards, nor revilers, nor swindlers, will inherit the kingdom of God." This passage states clearer than day that neither lady-men nor homosexuals will ever inherit the Kingdom of God. They are not Christians and to not be a Christian is to be in sin against God. Sin will not enter the Kingdom of God and thus both lady-men and homosexuals are singled out as sinful and not worthy of the Kingdom of God. Homosexuality is a disease that is swindling people out of their proper inheritance through Jesus Christ in the Kingdom of God. Unrepentant homosexuals are not to be trusted...especially around your children.

Lastly, I went to 1 Timothy 1:8-11 (NASB), "But we know that the Law is good, if one uses it lawfully, realizing the fact that law is not made for a righteous person, but for those who are lawless and rebellious, for the ungodly and sinners, for the unholy and profane, for those who kill their fathers or mothers, for murderers and immoral men and homosexuals and kidnappers and liars and perjurers, and whatever else is contrary to sound teaching, according to the glorious gospel of the blessed God, with which I have been entrusted." Paul states plainly that homosexuality is on par with murder, kidnapping, and all else that is contrary to God. God allowed these words to remain in his scripture...thus God believes the same thing. I do not see how you can believe anything that God says is like murder could not be considered a sin.

The Old Testament and the New Testament are very clear...homosexuality is a sin. Do not be fooled to think the battle is this clear, there is a homosexual agenda out there...often within the church...that is trying to make homosexuality into something acceptable. We must resist the lies of the homosexuals. They are the lies of the devil. We must keep them away from our children so as not to let them fall into their grasp. They are seeking to turn our children toward the devil. We must turn them away from our churches just like God does until they come to repentance. We pray they will.

2.

Though I have discarded much of what my elders taught me about socio-political issues, I am grateful I inherited love and strength that I could base new faith on throughout the pains of growth.

Senior Adult Day Keynote

The Rock Baptist Church

Rex, Georgia

June 15, 2003

Good Morning... What a pleasure it always is to be home at The Rock Baptist Church. For those who do not know me, my name is Jeffrey Kyle Hood. I am here today to reflect on some very important people in my life, most of whom are over the age of seventy. These are people who are able to transcend physical limitations and touch the very spirit nature of who we are. They shape us, mold us, and make us. They guide us so as to not hemorrhage gains already made and to continue a fast pace of achievement. Some go by the name grandparent or elder, but most have lived long enough to simply go by sage.

In Proverbs 4:23 (NASB) we are told, "Watch over your heart with all diligence, for from it flow the wellspring of life." I would like to thank the soon to be mentioned persons for turning my wellspring of life into a mighty thunderous river. You have shown me Christ and fought many battles alongside me in the pursuit of a more Christian existence. My elders have helped me to taste the sweetness of a life with Christ. These fine people are all here today...

Frances and Ray Hood and Jack and Gladys Dillard have been there since the beginning...changing diapers, playing all types of ball, and bestowing on me some of life's greatest lessons. With much zeal and determination, they have taught me the true meaning of the abundance and courage that comes with a life dedicated to Christ. They have taught me and shown me how to stand up for my beliefs in the face of a society that is lost and going to hell. They have taught me to resist the dangers of homosexuality, liberal politics, hippiism, and a whole host of other evils. They have truly taught me what it means to be both an American patriot and a Christian. Through their perseverance in their own lives, I now know what true faith is.

My grandfather Jack Dillard is battling bladder cancer. Though the battle is hard, my grandfather refuses to give up. The courage and tenacity he shows day in and day out gives me tremendous strength for facing adversity in this life. Granddaddy, you have always been my #1 supporter. I love you and will be deeply immersed in prayer for you. My grandmother Frances Hood is a rock in my life and in my family's life. She oozes confidence, tenacity, and strength everywhere she goes. I will never fear, because I know that she will always be with me. My grandmother Gladys Dillard has also been a constant companion. She has been a dear friend whom I have always been able to hold on to and share life with. Both of my grandmothers show me what it means to be a true Christian woman. I love, admire, and respect them endlessly. They have taught me what to look for when I seek my own wife. My grandfather Ray Hood is a silly man just like me and he has always taught me that love needs to be a little goofy sometimes. All of my grandparents have molded me into a young man desperately clinging to the things they have taught me and desperately seeking the Lord's guidance in my everyday life. I want to thank ya'll for all that I am and might ever hope to be.

Before I conclude, I also want to mention two other senior adults in the congregation who have been enormously influential in my life. First, I would like to thank Harmon Born. An esteemed and accomplished capitalist, Brother Harmon taught me in 12th Grade Sunday School the value of being a principled Christian. Brother, I knew the Lord's principles and was ready to face life when I graduated from high school due primarily to your teachings. Thank you... I also wanted to recognize the lady who changed my life forever, Lefa Hayes. Sister Lefa you might have forgotten this, but it was through your teachings of Christ's love in 4th Grade Sunday School that I came to desire to accept Jesus Christ as my personal lord and savior. Sister Lefa for your willingness to share the love of Jesus I am eternally indebted to you. Thank you for giving...

My life will never be the same based on the interactions I have had with the people I have mentioned. I pray that the Rock Baptist Church will never lose sight of the importance of its elders. This community of elders and senior adults has touched me and continues to touch me each time I am at home. I want to thank everyone in this room over the age of seventy...for being there and helping see me through. Thank you for investing in this church and all of our lives. You have successfully carried the cross of Christ valiantly and deserve to see your reward here in the land of the living... So, never let anyone put you away in a nursing home as if you have no value.

So, now let us press onward, upward, and forward with all deliberate speed in the spirit of these fine people...so that the Rock Baptist Church will continue to be a place where love is real and lives are changed forever.

Amen.

3.

I laughed loudly when I read this again...but this little devotion illustrates the reverence I was taught to carry for the Bible. I really thought I was helping all of the college students I was asked to give this devotion to. I am sure they thought I was a pious twit.

Read Your Bible

College Devotion

Auburn University

Auburn, Alabama

April 15, 2004

You can't go to heaven without reading your Bible. Jesus says in John 14:6 (NASB), "I am the way, and the truth, and the life." Jesus is the way...the only way. How are you going to know the only way of Jesus without the Bible? If you don't read the Bible then you are bound to believe a bunch of stuff that someone else made up...like all the other religions of the world. Paul, in 2 Timothy 3:16 (NASB), says, "ALL scripture is inspired by God..." What else do you know that claims in and of itself to be inspired by God? The Bible is God's word and if we want to know God then we have to listen to the word. Jesus says in John 1:1 (NASB), "In the beginning was the Word, and the Word was with God and the Word was God." Did you hear that? Jesus says that the Bible is God. Does God make mistakes? Of course not... Then there are no mistakes in the Bible. The Bible is perfect just like God...it is God. If you want to know God then you have to know your Bible. Read your Bible.

4.

I delivered this sermon on a college mission trip. The orphanage I spoke to was an evangelical Christian outfit that was always talking about God and Jesus. In my arrogance, I presumed that I had something to teach them about love. The truth of the matter is that they had much more to teach me than I them. I hustled through this talk to get to the invitation. In the evangelical world I grew up in…saving souls was about all that mattered. For all of its faults, this sermon does illustrate my growing desire to find a faith based primarily on love.

The Non-Perishability of Jesus/Love

Orphanage de Emmanuel Sunday Services

Guimmaca, Honduras

May 15, 2005

Good Morning! What a pleasure it is to join the people of Orphanage Emmanuel of Honduras. I love you. I love you. I love you. The immeasurable power of these words are absolutely stunning and unbelievable. In John chapter 3 verse 16 (NASB) we find Jesus sending us one big, "I love you." "For God so loved the world, that He gave His only begotten Son, that whoever believes in Him shall not perish, but have eternal life." We all hunger for love. We have to have something more than the mundane everyday boringness of life. The problem is that the temporal love we experience daily is fleeting and quickly departing. It is here today and gone tomorrow. Temporal love does not last.

The only love that is non-perishable is the love of Jesus Christ. This, my dear brethren, is a love we can rest secure in. Such love reminds me of the old short tale of Zacheuss in Luke 19... Jesus was walking through that densely populated town and just so happened to look up into the trees. There he saw a wee little man down on his luck and in search of a love connection. Zaccheuss is one of the most representative figures we find in the entire Bible. We all find ourselves at one time or another strung out, down on our luck, and in search of a love connection. Zacheus represents all of our individual searches for love. Like Zacheuss, we all know that if we can get one glimpse of the love of Jesus then we will be ok. If we could just see him... Zacheuss climbed a tree...

The distraction in this life is to live for something beside the love of Jesus...mainly human desire. We go to great lengths to fill the hole in our heart with temporal things. We forget the Bible's warning in Matthew chapter 6 verse 21 (NASB), "where your treasure is, there your heart will be also." Do we want our lives filled with things that are perishable or imperishable? Love is not fleeting like the things of this world. If we can just get a glimpse of the Savior then maybe we might know the love that is imperishable...

Jesus saw Zacheus and cried out to him... The only way we can experience true everlasting love is to hurry down the tree of false promises and run to see Jesus. When Zacheus ran to him, Jesus received him gladly. He will embrace me or you gladly no matter what our place or status in life. While Zacheus ran, others grumbled. How many of you know about finding and cherishing something good while everyone around you grumbles? Selfish people don't want others to be happy. They want everyone to be in the same miserable boat. So when someone gets or does something good, they grumble... They are joy/love takers and that is all they know how to do. Whatever love they get, they want to keep it all for themselves. The problem is that when you try to keep love and fail to give it away...then it starts to burn out. When you accept the big love of Jesus and give it away then you have something that can go global. When Jesus died on the cross he showed us what big love is... "Greater love has no one than this, that one lay down his life for his friends" (John 15:13 NASB). Zaccheus came down to embrace and grab at that type of love. Where are you today? We are all sinners in desperate need of that type of big love that we can grow by giving it away.

In a world of darkness and desolation, we must find this big love to light our way. Paul tells us in 1 Corinthians chapter 13 that if we don't have love then we are nothing. Think of what your life would be if you did not have love. Many of you today are orphans… What would it be like if you were living on the street and didn't have this generous type of facility to love and take care of you? These people here love you. They know Jesus and that is why they are doing this for you. They love you. Can you imagine living in isolation or in the garbage dumps like many orphans in Guatemala do? You should be thankful for what you have! You have the love of Jesus caring for you. If we didn't have love we wouldn't make it, but unfortunately many of you are failing to accept the love of Jesus…

There is only one permanent and lasting way to experience the big love of Jesus Christ…by embracing and holding it. The way to embrace and hold it is by asking Jesus, the big love, into your heart. Can you imagine receiving a love that is not selfish? We always think about ourselves… Since old Adam took a bite out of the old apple tree we have always been selfish, but this selfless love conquers everything. Can you imagine a love that cannot be shot, mutilated, beat down, wiped out, burned up, or made to experience any other type of destruction? This love never fails! Jesus never fails! When you are in Him you never fail! This world will eventually end. All things will pass away, but Jesus, the big love, the embodiment of love, will remain… Don't believe this type of love exists? Fine…I will prove it. Look into my heart. Jesus is burning right in there. Jesus, the embodiment of love, guides me each and every day. Jesus is mine. Jesus is yours. Love is yours unconditionally if you accept it. You need Jesus and so do you, you, you, you, you, and every single last one of you. We all need Jesus. We do not have a chance without Jesus. According to Ephesians chapter 3 verses 17-19 (NASB), Jesus came "so that Christ might dwell in our hearts through faith; and that you, being rooted and grounded in love, may be able to comprehend with all the saints what is the breadth and length and height and depth, and to know the love of Christ which surpasses knowledge, that you may be filled up to all the fullness of God."

We must know this love that is beyond all comprehension... We must find this love... We must show this love to others... We have got to follow Paul's command in 1 Corinthians chapter 14 verse 1 to pursue love. We pursue love by getting down out of the tree, embracing Jesus, and giving away the big love that he has given us. We have got to get that big love...we have got to make it a part of our lives...we have got to grow it by giving it away... We live in a world of greed, corruption, crime, meanness, selfishness, and all other evils... Send the light of the big love of Jesus Christ! There is no way out of the darkness apart from the big love of Jesus. We scream out the words of the prophet Micah (7:8 NASB), "though I dwell in darkness, the Lord is a light for me." People are in darkness! Send the light of love! People are drowning in their problems! Send the light of love! People are sick! Send the light of love! People are in desperate need of a savior! Send the light of love! In this wasteland of sin! Send the light of love! Jesus in Matthew chapter 11 verses 28-30

(NASB) said, "Come to me, all who are weary and heavy-laden, and I will give you rest. Take my yoke upon you and learn from me, for I am gentle and humble in heart, and you will find rest for your souls. For my yoke is easy and my burden is light." Come and accept the light burden of the big love of Jesus Christ.

The burden he gives you is the light of love...accept it. If you are here this morning and have never accepted the light of love then now is the time to embrace Jesus. If you feel like you have turned away from the light of the big love of Jesus then today is your day to turn back. Maybe you don't know where you are...well to you I say turn toward the light of love and you will never forget it. The Lord wishes that none will perish... Do not wait. This is the Lord's day. Salvation is upon us. Love is upon us. The light of the big love of Jesus is free...come... While the music plays...please...don't you tarry...you come...

Brothers and sisters in this wasteland desert of poverty, malnutrition, and struggle we have found an oasis of grace...today we welcome five new members of the Kingdom of Heaven. I can't wait until we all get there...

Amen.

5.

I am a doubter. I have always been a doubter. Evangelicals don't give much room for doubt...so I felt like it was my job to prove to myself and others the resurrection actually happened. Talks like these worked for a little while...but I eventually just got depressed.

The Life, Death, and Resurrection Dissected

Bald Rock Community Easter Sunrise Service

Wadley, Alabama

April 16, 2006

He is risen! Hallelujah! Hallelujah! Jesus is risen! Jesus Christ is risen indeed!

Welcome to the never-ending story of love... Because Jesus Christ is risen we know that love cannot be killed or entombed. This love flows out in three distinct parts...

The first flowing of Christ's love rests in whom Jesus Christ said he was when he was here on this earth. In John 14:6 (NASB), we find Jesus declaring, "I am the way, and the truth, and the life; no one comes to the Father but through me." This was and is a startling proclamation. Jesus declares that he was and is the Son of God...but not only this...he declares himself to be the only way to God. That means none of the other religions can get you to God...only Jesus. Our knowledge of Jesus rests in our affirmation of his affirmation of himself. In Matthew 16 (NASB), when Jesus asks Peter who he considers Jesus to be...Peter demurs and says..."Some say John the Baptist; and others, Elijah; but still others, Jeremiah, or one of the prophets." That answer didn't work for Peter and it ain't going to work for us. Jesus questions Peter again, "But who do you say that I am?" This is when Peter shines and we would do well to follow his lead: "You are the Christ, the Son of the Living God." When Jesus himself asks you who you say that he is... How are you going to reply? Well, if you want to embrace the love of Jesus that knows no boundaries or death then you must say, "You are the way, you are the truth, and you are the life...you are the Christ, the very Son of the Living God." We first find his beautiful love in his proclamation of divinity, but the story does not end there and we are able to go deeper in his love through the second distinct outflow...his death.

The resurrection of Jesus does not occur without the death of Jesus. The death is a phenomenally important part of this magical narrative. However, we must understand our part in the death first. Jesus died for our sins. This means that we nailed him to the tree. It was our selfish desires that that made the blood pour out from his hands, feet, side, head, and eventually made life leave his body. Jesus could have avoided this fate and we would have still been dead in our sins BUT real love always chooses death in order to save others. To save us from our condemnation Jesus placed himself on the cross. In agony, he cried out, "Father, forgive them; for they do not know what they are doing." Too often we are taught that Jesus' cry for forgiveness was for those in Jerusalem who had just persecuted and crucified him. While partially true, this statement too quickly delivers absolution to us. You see it was our sins that put Jesus on the cross and our sins that killed him… In dying for us, Jesus, perhaps not knowing how the story would end or if anyone would ever accept him, took an extravagant risk to show just how much he loves us. Jesus died to show his love, but praise God, the story doesn't end here.

The third and most glorious part of Jesus' extravagant love is his defiance of death and his resurrection into the embodiment of love eternal overflowing. Satan could have sworn that he had won…he was probably telling all of his demons that he had really beat God this time…but Hallelujah! Jesus loves us way too much for that. As we look out over the sunrise with trees glistening and swaying, birds chirping and singing, little creatures stirring, imagine what it must have been like for those women who, in addition to hearing all the noises we are hearing, also saw the empty linen, radiant angels, and eventually Jesus. Later, Jesus appeared to the disciples who had failed him just a few days prior. The love of Jesus does not end with earthly failures but arises to live forever.

To complete the saga of love...Jesus gave a command, instructions, and a promise. "Go therefore and make disciples of all nations, baptizing them in the name of the Father and the Son and the Holy Spirit, teaching them to observe all that I commanded you; and lo I am with you always, even to the end of the age" (Matthew 28:19 NASB). Those who do not believe in the resurrection only have to look at the disciples' response to what they saw and heard. These guys went from hiding in an upper room to dying the deaths of martyrs...having preached the Gospel of Jesus all over the known world. The greatest proof of the resurrection is the response to meeting the everlasting love of Jesus. So as we watch the sun/the son come up in our eyes and in our hearts...let us remember that we have a responsibility to take the everlasting love of Jesus to the ends of the Earth so that the love will shine brightly the world over. Let us pray...

God of light. Shine bright. Guide us in your will and in your way. May we be the generation who takes your love to the ends of the Earth. Thank you for your death and resurrection. Now, let us leave this place resting assured in your hope, your promises, and in your love... In the name of the Father, Son, and Holy Spirit... Amen, amen, and amen...

6.

This is a good example of the fire and brimstone evangelical theology I believed for most of my early life. I decided that Independence Day would be a good day to bring down God's fireworks. I believed that the devil had taken the church, the community, and the nation hostage...and that we needed to do some serious soul-searching and pray that God would save us. I was taught very early on that no matter the issue, God was on the side of the United States. On a quick side note, I had been ordained by The Rock Baptist Church about a month prior. Now, God and a Southern Baptist church had placed a stamp of approval on my ministry. I also have no idea why I used the illustration about my former girlfriend.

Rediscovering the Passion for Our Community and Nation

Wadley Baptist Church

Wadley, Alabama

Independence Day 2006

2 Chronicles 7:13-16 (NASB)

"If I shut up the heavens so that there is no rain, or if I command the locust to devour the land, or if I send pestilence among My people, and My people who are called by My name humble themselves and pray and seek My face and turn from their wicked ways, then I will hear from heaven, will forgive their sin and will heal their land. Now My eyes will be open and My ears attentive to the prayers offered in this place. For now I have chosen and consecrated this house so that my Name may be there forever, and My eyes and My heart will be there perpetually."

Good morning! What a beautiful thing to be present with the people of God. This morning we are going to tackle a pivotal question...

Where has the passion for sharing the Gospel of Jesus Christ gone in this church and in the many other churches throughout our land?

Passion for sharing the Gospel of Jesus Christ is substantive. It means something. How often do we talk about things that mean nothing? I look around at our church and other churches arguing about stuff that means nothing. At this church...lately...all we have wanted to talk about is what color the pews are going to be... Stuff. How much are we going to pay the pastor? Stuff. Who is going to be the Sunday School Director? Stuff. What happened to the passionate desire to share the soul-stirring truths of the Gospel of Jesus Christ in Wadley, Alabama? Locally...the devil is at work distracting us from the very issue that matters...the salvation of our neighbors. Nationally...the same is true. Everyone wants to talk about homosexuality. That is all any churchperson wants to talk about. Folks, locally and nationally we are off on side streets used to distract us from our main purpose...the passionate sharing of the Gospel of Jesus Christ.

I am disgusted by all of these health and wealth preachers out there... Joel Osteen and his cohorts promise all of our worldly desires but fail to talk to us about the life-saving Gospel of Jesus Christ. You can get you a Cadillac Deville...but unfortunately you can't drive it to heaven.

We have got to do some soul-searching folks! I know about soul-searching this week. For some time, I have struggled concerning my relationship with Olivia. She has treated me like dirt...but I have been afraid to be alone. I have prayed for strength. This week as I was examining my future...I asked myself a question: Where is the passion in your own life? Where is the passion in your relationship with Olivia? The truth is that both passions were non-existent. I broke up with Olivia last week...the passion was gone and there were other matters that deserved my attention. When you begin to examine your own life...you often realize areas were passion is gone. Where is the passion gone in your own life? I know your passion for sharing the Gospel of Jesus Christ is gone or we would have more people in this church. Where is the passion? Where is your passion?

On this day, we must realize that we have failed to hold up our end of the passion bargain. Jesus passionately gave his life for us and we have failed to give our lives passionately back to him. How do we save our communities? How do we save our nation? How do we find our passion?

In 2 Chronicles 7:14, we find God speaking to Solomon about the redemption of the nation Israel. In these next few verses, God instructs Solomon on where to place his passions if he wants to save his community, his nation, and himself.

In verse 14, God commands Solomon to get the people to humble themselves before the Lord.

We are not a humble people... We live in a culture that demands bigger...because we know that bigger is always better. Just look to the mega churches...that is where the real spirituality is... Right? We are a people confused by our pride.

At my home church...the Rock Baptist Church in Rex, Georgia...we had a lady who asked the pastor if he could use more stories and less scriptures in his sermons. What audacity?!?! Does this woman or any of us think that we are above using God's word in sermons? What good is a Christian Church that does not preach God's word? The truth of the matter is there is no good in it and it shouldn't be called a church...but rather a social club. What else is a church that does not stand on the word of God? We have journeyed far from our core passion of the Gospel of Jesus Christ...

As verse 14 commands...we must pray and seek God's face. We must have passion for our relationships with Jesus Christ.

God also commands Solomon to tell the people to turn from their wicked ways. Unfortunately, we love our wickedness more than we love the people who need to hear the Gospel of Jesus Christ. There is no question that the largest cause of atheism in the world today is Christians who live a life contrary to what the Gospel commands.

God tells us in 1 Peter 5:8 (NASB), "Be of sober spirit, be on the alert. Your adversary, the devil, prowls around like a roaring lion, seeking someone to devour."

The devil is having a feast in Wadley, Alabama and in the United States of America.

Let me tell you something folks... If Jesus was to let his vengeance loose on our community and nation...it would make Soddom and Gommorah seem like an appetizer. We must stop our wickedness...the world needs us.

If Christians would just live like Christians then we would quickly see the harvest of our world for Christ.

In our nation we must follow the old adage, "Love the sinner hate the sin." We just hate people... How is it possible to talk with someone about Jesus if you hate them? If we will develop a passion for sinners...then we will be the vessels God uses to win our nation back for Jesus Christ.

God also promises Solomon that if he does these things...then God will hear from heaven and heal their land. We have got to humble ourselves and return to our main mission...saving souls. This mission will take courage...but we have got all the strength we need with Jesus on our side. We begin with the words of C.S. Lewis ringing in our ears, "Courage is not just a virtue. It is the virtue."

I am so tired of churches fighting about social issues more than they are fighting for the souls of their countrymen. We need courage to win this nation for Jesus! We have got to start fighting for souls! If you ask any number of people if they believe in school prayer...they will jump and shout...but ask them to share the gospel with their neighbor...they backtrack. We had a rally for school prayer in Wadley, Alabama two weeks ago...many of you were there...but where were you a week later when we asked you to join us in going to visit with your neighbors? We have got to regain our passion for winning souls... If we did...then there would be no need for school prayer…as God would heal our land from top to bottom. We must regain our passion!

In 2 Chronicles 7:13 we hear of great tragedies that begin to devour the land. Solomon is told to pray. As the enormity of our task here in Wadley, Alabama and in our nation begins to overtake us…we must pray… We must humble ourselves in prayer as a community and as a nation.

On this Independence Day…for the sake of Wadley, Alabama and the United States of America…we must rediscover our passion for winning the lost and allow God to begin to work to heal our land.

On July 4, 1776 the signers of the Declaration of Independence pledged to each other their lives and their scared honor. On this day we must do the same…

The founders of our nation were willing to give their fortunes and good names for each other. On this day we must do the same…

Will you this day pray and give yourself so that this community might know Christ?

Will you this day pray and give yourself so that this nation might know Christ?

Look deep within yourself for the passion...

I lament in the words of Revelation 2:4...that we have left our first love.

Return to your first love church. Return to Jesus.

2 Chronicles 7:14 (NASB):

If, "My people who are called by My name humble themselves and pray and seek My face and turn from their wicked ways, then I will hear from heaven, will forgive their sin and will heal their land."

Let us pray... Today, God, I pray that the battle to redeem our nation will begin right here in each of our hearts. May we shun these distractions and rediscover our passion. God, we pray that you will accomplish in this church and in this nation your words of 2 Chronicles 7: 15-16 (NASB): "Now My eyes will be open and My ears attentive to the prayers offered in this place. For now I have chosen and consecrated this house so that my Name may be there forever, and My eyes and My heart will be there perpetually." God, may today be the beginning of you reigniting our passions for this community and this nation. May today be the beginning of the end of the reign of wickedness and the beginning of a passion more fiery than the world has never known.

Amen.

7.

I credit a recovery program at Cloverdale Baptist Church for igniting in me a passion for the oppressed and the marginalized. I had never read Matthew 25:31-46 before I encountered this program. I met folks who were homeless, sick, strung out, and in desperate need of help. I started to invite people to stay in my home. I got myself into a few hairy situations...not the least of which occurred when a man confessed to a murder in my apartment before dozing off to sleep on my couch. Though I was still every bit an evangelical, I was beginning to realize that the message of Jesus was about more than just those society deemed safe and privileged.

Passion for the Least

Cloverdale Baptist Church

October 1, 2006

First Baptist Church of East Point

October 15, 2006

Matthew 25:31-46 (NASB)

"But when the Son of Man comes in His glory, and all the angels with Him, then He will sit on His glorious throne. All the nations will be gathered before Him; and He will separate them from one another, as the shepherd separates the sheep from the goats; and He will put the sheep on His right, and the goats on the left." "Then the King will say to those on His right, 'Come, you who are blessed of My Father, inherit the kingdom prepared for you from the foundation of the world. For I was hungry, and you gave Me *something* to eat; I was thirsty, and you gave Me *something* to drink; I was a stranger, and you invited Me in; naked, and you clothed Me; I was sick, and you visited Me; I was in prison, and you came to Me.' Then the righteous will answer Him, 'Lord, when did we see You hungry, and feed You, or thirsty, and give You *something* to drink? And when did we see You a stranger, and invite You in, or naked, and clothe You? When did we see You sick, or in prison, and come to You?" The King will answer and say to them, 'Truly I say to you, to the extent that you did it to one of these brothers of Mine, *even* the least *of them*, you did it to Me.'" "Then He will also say to those on His left, 'Depart from Me, accursed ones, into the eternal fire which has been prepared for the devil and his angels; for I was hungry, and you gave Me *nothing* to eat; I was thirsty, and you gave Me nothing to drink; I was a stranger, and you did not invite Me in; naked, and you did not clothe Me; sick, and in prison, and you did not visit Me.' Then they themselves also will answer, 'Lord, when did we see You hungry, or thirsty, or a stranger, or naked, or sick, or in prison, and did not take care of You?' Then He will answer them, 'Truly I say to you, to the extent that you did not do it to one of the least of these, you did not do it to Me.' These will go away into eternal punishment, but the righteous into eternal life."

Until I arrived at Cloverdale Baptist Church, I never knew the contents of Matthew 25. In the culture I grew up in, this passage would have been a secondary concern to getting people saved. I never considered that Jesus might have said that a concern for the least was a primary component of salvation. In seeing the persons who have attended the recovery program at Cloverdale Baptist Church, I have realized that salvation is a broad concept. Salvation is not just about saving one's self...it is about saving others. Saving others does not just consist of a prayer...but seeking to redeem the whole of an individual. In the passion, Jesus Christ sacrificially gave his life for all of us. In our passion, may we sacrificially give our lives to the least. Our passion takes place in three forms.

In our individual lives we must be prepared to sacrifice. One of the initial forms of sacrifice we must engage in is an opening of ourselves to the pain of others. When we open ourselves up and let our emotions get involved with others then we open ourselves up to the possibility of tremendous pain. The scriptures reveal that those who set themselves on the path of sacrifice usually die a death of sacrifice. Jesus in John 15:13 (NASB) tells us, "Greater love has no one than this, that one lay down his life for his friends." Are you prepared to open yourself up and lay down your life for the least? This is what Jesus calls us to. The second form of sacrifice the individual must engage in is the sacrifice of time. You have to open up your schedule if you want to serve the least. You have to create windows in which you expect nothing but to exist with the folks who Jesus called us to exist with. Don't go to the soup kitchen, go to the streets and exist to relieve the burdens of the people who live there. The third form of sacrifice comes from the pocket book. Jesus told the rich man...and let me assure you...if you own a house or a car...you are the rich man...in Luke 18:22 (NASB), "Sell all that you possess and distribute it to the poor, and you shall have treasure in heaven; and come, follow Me." Maybe we should sell this beautiful building we are presently in to provide for money for the poor in the area. Maybe we should take off our rings and watches and give them to the poor. God is always calling you to a deeper level of sacrifice. The passion of the self takes place in three forms in one's heart/emotions, time, and finances. It is time that we follow Jesus and sacrifice all three of these components of our lives for the least.

In our church life we must be prepared to sacrifice. There is no question that the current recovery program you are doing is an incredibly positive phenomenon. You are reaching persons that no other church in the area is reaching. There is, however, more to do. The first area of sacrifice that God is calling you to is that sacrifice of time and energy. One night a week is good...but it is not enough. What if you had a feeding ministry every night of the week? The building would not be able to contain the people who would enter these walls. You are capable of it. Why not?

I know the main reason you are scared to do a sleeping ministry...you are scared that the least will destroy this building. John says in 1 John 4:18 (NASB), "There is no fear in love." So...open your hearts as you open your doors. People need a place to sleep and you have a place to give them. Is it your desire to let Jesus sleep out in the cold? There is also a need to give of this church financially. You have an ability to do so much more. Open up the church coffers and let the people eat. Open up the church coffers and let the people shower. Open up the church coffers and let the people survive. Why are you holding back? The least needs you. Jesus needs you.

In closing, may we be Christians who recognize that salvation is more than a prayer. May we realize that we are needed for emotional, financial, and other critical support. The least are shouting in the streets begging for your support. Will you open your hearts, doors, and pocketbooks to Jesus?

If you have heard the message of the least today and want to follow Jesus...as the music plays you come.

Amen.

8.

Like many other evangelicals, I had an obsession with John Winthrop and his message that the United States is to be the city set on a hill spoken of in Matthew 5:14. I consistently preached the need to save the nation. I often forgot that Jesus came to save the world. I can feel myself building on my experiences at Cloverdale Baptist Church and moving in a more open direction in this sermon. I wanted the Rock Baptist Church, the church of my youth, to be a part of meeting the needs of the community. I thought that we could combine evangelical theology with cutting edge social outreach to change the world. It was very meaningful to me when we prayed for the community on the front steps of the church after the service. I felt like these words could be the difference…

Happy New Year!: Now Let's Light the Way…

The Rock Baptist Church

New Year's Service

Rex, Georgia

January 1, 2007

I promise I won't take up all of your new year…

I begin this morning with Paul's words to Timothy…there is no need to be timid or hesitant for we are empowered by the very blood of Jesus Christ… I claim this empowerment and I invite you to come with me as we approach the throne of grace together.

I have good news for all of you today. Jesus is alive in 2007! Can I get a hallelujah? In the beginning, God said let there be light and there was light. The Genesis account of creation is a magical dazzling array of light. Light is an entity that brightens our lives and directs our paths. Have you ever got a lightened word from the Lord? I have. I actually got it right here in this sanctuary. Indeed, it was many years ago that I was sitting on the right side of the sanctuary midway back when a bright light shown through the window and warmed my soul. I am sure that many of you have had similar experiences in this sanctuary. For me, that light spoke…reminding me of Jesus' presence in my life and in the life of this church.

John 1 verses 4 and 5 speak to us that Jesus is life and his life gives light to all men…Jesus' light shines through all darkness and darkness can never extinguish the light. You see this light…the impenetrable light of Jesus Christ…is very important for us to think about as we ponder the future. If the Rock Baptist Church clings to this light then it has a future…if it does not, then it does not have a future. Jesus is the flashlight that guides us through the darkness of life. As we begin 2007 this morning, let us carefully examine our and the Rock Baptist Church's responsibilities to Jesus Christ through the subject of light.

I would like to share with you three specific well-lighted points about Christians and light.

My first point is that we have a responsibility as Christians to be a light for Jesus Christ in our nation. Jesus states in Matthew 5:14 (NASB), "You are the light of the world. A city set on a hill cannot be hidden." In 1630, as the Puritans sailed towards the shores of what was to eventually become Massachusetts, John Winthrop took the words of Jesus and adapted them to his context...

> For we must consider that we shall be as a city upon a hill. The eyes of all people are upon us. So that if we shall deal falsely with our God in this work we have undertaken...we shall be made a story and a by-word throughout the world. We shall open the mouths of enemies to speak evil of the ways of God... We shall shame the faces of many of God's worthy servants, and cause their prayers to be turned into curses upon us til we be consumed out of the good land whither we are going.

Today, we have left Winthrop's vision of what this land we call America can be and turned towards darkness. We have turned away from God and turned to the dark vices of homosexuality, arrogance, government assistance, abortion, socialism, drugs, and other forms of rampant immorality. We have allowed God to be taken out of our government and our hearts.

As Christians we must do something! This is a call to arms. We must fight for all that we believe and hold dear. We must fight for the very person of Jesus Christ! Together we scream, "Cast out oh evil darkness! Stop you perpetrators of evil and malice! God is here and he has a plan for our country!" We are spiritually sick. Can you feel it? This is not a Republican or Democratic problem or a liberal or conservative problem... This is a God problem! The sickness of the encroaching immorality that surrounds us can only be solved by the soul saving blood of Jesus Christ.

Praise God, today us Christian soldiers here at the Rock Baptist Church enlist ourselves in the war to win our nation back for Jesus Christ. For, brothers and sisters, only a return back to that magical city on a hill will solve our nation's problems and cure our societal ills. We have got to get back to Jesus.

A week ago, we were reminded of the birth of our dear savior in Bethlehem. Isaiah, in chapter 9 verse 6 (NASB), prophesied, "the government will rest on his shoulders." Does our government rest on his shoulders? Praise God we will make it so! The first step is to take the light of Jesus to the highways and halls of our nation and government. When we do…2 Chronicles chapter 7 verse 14 (NASB) tells us the result…

> If, "My people who are called by My name humble themselves and pray and seek My face and turn from their wicked ways, then I will hear from heaven, will forgive their sin and will heal their land."

Praise God, let it begin today! Edmund Burke said, "all that is necessary for evil to prosper is for good people to do nothing." Christian brothers and sisters, we have got to stop doing nothing. Our nation needs us to light the way…with our ballots, our boots, our prayers, our causes, and our lives. Get up! Get up! Get up! Be that light that our nation so desperately needs in 2007!

My second point is this… We must also be a light to the community of Rex in 2007. Our community is infested with crime, drugs, gangs, prostitution, homosexuality, and all other sorts of dark activities and practices. Just a month ago there was a double homicide in Rex Park. Where is this church? Did you contact the families? Go to the funeral home? Think about the ramifications of the Rock Baptist Church becoming known as a place that recklessly loves this community…

Anybody read the Clayton News Daily lately? The top story is about the rise of gangs and the death of a police officer. Last Wednesday in Morrow there were two homicides in one night… Our community is screaming for the light. Where are we? Are we going to be a part of the light or the darkness? To remain silent is to be a part of the darkness. Jesus in John 8:12 (NASB) declared, "I am the Light of the world; he who follows Me will not walk in the darkness, but will have the Light of life." We have the eternal light to give to our community… Will you give our community the light of Christ? Now is the time to fling open your doors and invite the folks in this community to this place of refuge. We are the shelter from the darkness. We are the lighthouse.

In the ancient Roman Empire, when plagues and natural disasters hit, people were known to flee to the cities seeking help and care from Christians. You see, church…in ancient Rome Christians were known to provide aid to anyone seeking it no matter their race, color, or ethnicity, no matter how desperate their situation, no matter there economic status, and no matter what affliction they face. This morning you need to ask yourself if you are the Christians of ancient Rome… You should be.

Jesus said in Matthew 25:45 (NASB), "…to the extent you did not do it to one of the least of these, you did not do it unto me." On this first day of 2007, we have the opportunity to be the Body of Christ in this community that ultimately connects so much with the least that we like Christ become them. Are you willing to go that far? Are you willing to take on their pain and their hurts? Are you willing to be Jesus? If we do nothing...we will stand before Jesus one day and answer for such shortcomings...to the extent which you failed the least of these you failed me...

If we do nothing in this community where will the light come from? Listen church...we must be the distributor of light for this community. We must love this community in order to save it.

If we become known for our love...then the walls of this church will not be able to contain the masses of red, yellow, black, brown, and white faces who walk through these doors.

My third and final point includes five things that we must remember as we foster the light of Jesus in ourselves from Isaiah 43 and Jeremiah 29:11 (NASB).

First, we must remember that we are created by grand design. In 43:1, God says I am "He who formed you."

Second, we must remember that we were created to seek God. In 43:1, God says "I have called you by name; you are Mine!"

Third, we must not forget that God is protecting us and he wants us to succeed. In 43:2-3, God says, "When you pass through the waters, I will be with you; And through the rivers, they will not overflow you. When you walk through the fire, you will not be scorched, Nor will the flame burn you. For I am the LORD your God..."

Fourth, we must remember that God created us to be bold and adventurous for his causes. Jeremiah 29:11 tells us that God declares, "For I know the plans that I have for you,' declares the LORD, 'plans for welfare and not for calamity to give you a future and a hope."

Fifth and finally, God has created us for eternity. Isaiah 43:25 tells us that, "I, even I, am the one who wipes out your transgressions for My own sake, And I will not remember your sins." You are created to be sinless and to love others. GO!

Church, on this the first day of 2007, may we make a commitment to stay focused on these five points and live together in community for Jesus. Let us each individually be the light that Jesus calls us to be.

In conclusion, in this new year of 2007, let us remember our country, our community, and spiritually ourselves. We must hold to biblical principles so as to never extinguish the flame of Christ in this community. If it is going to be church...it is up to us. May the light of Jesus be our only focus in 2007. Follow the message of Ephesians 5:8 (NASB), "You were formerly darkness, but now you are Light in the

Lord; walk as children of Light." So start stepping, church... Be the light our community, nation, and our world so desperately needs. GO!

As the invitation approaches if you have never embraced the light of Jesus Christ you come...or if you are looking for a church home you come...I can tell you that this is an amazing group of believers about to do amazing things in Rex, Georgia. Whatever God calls you to do...do it...you will never be sorry.

(After the invitation, the congregation proceeds out to the front of the church where I close the service in prayer...)

Jesus as we hear the cars go by and listen to the whirling of life all around us...grant us the courage to go and be the difference in Rex, in the United States, and throughout this little vessel we call Earth. Help us to love as you love. Help us to think as you think. Help us to live as you live. Incarnate yourself mightily Lord so that we will be the light needed to transform the darkness. We are your people and forever yours. In the name of the God that is love, the Son that is grace, and the Spirit that is brilliant transformational magic. Amen.

Go now in the light of Jesus!

9.

I had just started school at the Southern Baptist Theological Seminary when I came back to my home church to deliver this sermon. This is an attempt at what is called expository preaching, popular amongst evangelicals, where the text is the only vehicle for the sermon. I use the passage to spout out normal evangelical lines against the culture and encourage faithful outreach in the church. What most of my evangelical comrades and I neglected to realize was that there was something deficient in our basic theological outlook on the world...as we saw ourselves existing in judgment of the world, not with the world.

These are the Days of Elijah: Beholding the Power of God as We Allow Him to Consume Our Lives in a Community of Change

Sunday Worship

The Rock Baptist Church

February 2007

Good morning, Rock Baptist Church. It is always pleasure to come home. This is my home. Now, together let us look to the book from which our help comes...God's holy word...the Bible. I will be expositing and studying 1 Kings 18: 17-40 (NASB).

In 1 Kings 18:17, King Ahab senses Elijah approaching and shouts out, "Is this you, you troubler of Israel?"

Elijah is called the troubler of Israel. What are you called? When was the last time one of you was called a troublemaker? I am going to assume that for most of you it has been quite some time. Why? We are followers of a troublemaker. The message of Jesus was always controversial and troubled those who heard it. Where is our strong stand for the gospel of the troublemaker? It is time for people in a dark and dying world to look at us and say... "Is that you, troubler of Rex?" "Is that you, troubler of Georgia?" "Is that you, troubler of the United States of America?" Are you ready to become a troublemaker?

These are the days of Elijah!

In 1 Kings 18:20, as Elijah prepares for the coming showdown with the hundreds of prophets of Baal he beckons the people, "How long *will* you hesitate between two opinions? If the LORD is God, follow Him; but if Baal, follow him."

Elijah refused to move. He was all in. The Rock Baptist Church needs people who are all in. Elijah stood on the mountaintop and declared the truth of God. We need a body of believers who will firmly stand on this granite piece of land in Rex, Georgia and proclaim, "Thus saith the LORD!" Are you scared? Elijah was willing to stand entirely alone. He took his position in his community? Have you taken yours? May the words of the Rock Baptist Church be: here I stand...I can do no other. Are you ready to stand?

These are the days of Elijah!

In 1 Kings 18:23, we realize very quickly that Elijah has prepared for his battle with the prophets of Baal and has a plan, "Now let them give us two oxen; and let them choose one ox for themselves and cut it up, and place it on the wood, but put no fire *under it*; and I will prepare the other ox and lay it on the wood, and I will not put a fire *under it.*"

Elijah had a plan to tackle the circumstances around him. Do you? How can we expect to transform this community without a plan? We want God to show up...but sometimes I am afraid that you all left the bulls at home. What do we need to work on in order to get ourselves prepared to interact with the community? This church is mostly white. The community is mostly black. Wouldn't it be a good move to start striking up relationships with people of different races in the community? We need to be prepared for God to show up. This means that we begin to train ourselves as to what it means to be a multiethnic and multiracial church. There is work to be done. Are you ready to move?

These are the days of Elijah!

In 1 Kings 18:24 Elijah declares, "Then you call on the name of your god, and I will call on the name of the LORD, and the God who answers by fire, He is God."

Rock Baptist Church, are you ready for God to answer by fire? The thought of God answering with fire can be a little frightening. It disrupts our comfort and moves us to places of fresh overwhelming experiences. When God shows up God is going to show out. Are you ready for God to show up? A few questions might help to determine your readiness... What is comfortable for you? What are you afraid of? It is time to let go of such things and allow the God of fire to do his work. Are you ready for the fire Rock Baptist Church?

These are the days of Elijah!

In 1 Kings 18: 27, "It came about at noon, that Elijah mocked them and said, 'Call out with a loud voice, for he is a god; either he is occupied or gone aside, or is on a journey, or perhaps he is asleep and needs to be awakened.'"

Elijah mocked the Prophets of Baal. So often we as American Christians are terrified at what our culture might think of us or worried that we might not be accepted. We format our worship and church life to fit the culture's needs. We buy our kids all the latest stuff and we go see all the latest films. In the process, we attempt to legitimize Jesus for the culture. He was just a man. He was just a good guy. People don't really rise from the dead, do they? We give so much away to be accepted by a culture that is not going to accept us. Then we turn to Dr. Phil, Joel Osteen, and Oprah to try to figure out what is wrong with our children. Surprisingly...they don't have any answers. When are we going to learn to stop standing around like pieces of Jell-O? When are we going to stand tall against the culture and mock its deficiencies rather than join in? We, like Elijah, must look past the degraded culture and to the hills from whenceforth our fiery help comes. If necessary, we must be willing to stand against the culture alone... People all around us are worried about the most basic questions of life and instead of giving them answers...we make concessions. Feel the spirit of Elijah Rock Baptist Church... Stand tall! Stand tall! Stand tall! Give them the fiery Gospel of Our Lord!

These are the days of Elijah!

Elijah is standing patiently by in verses 28 and 29 waiting on the prophets of Baal: "So they cried with a loud voice and cut themselves according to their custom with swords and lances until the blood gushed out on them. When midday was past, they raved until the time of the offering of the *evening* sacrifice; but there was no voice, no one answered, and no one paid attention.."

Elijah knew that there was no other answer but God and he waited patiently for the prophets of Baal to give out. There was a confidence about Elijah and the supreme answer that he knew he provided to the numerous questions of his society. When was the last time that you had such confidence in the answer that is Jesus? Everyone in our culture is looking to pop psychology and feelings-based culture to provide answers to the questions and issues of homosexuality, poverty, depression, selfishness, drugs, gangs, violence, and hate. Many of you are caught in this same boat of looking everywhere else but Jesus for the answers to the questions of our time. When are you going to have the confidence of Elijah? When are you going to stand before the numerous false prophets of our time and declare Jesus as the one and only answer that matters? There is a void in these United States... There is a void in this town of Rex... We must step into that void and prophesy... Behold the power the fire of the living God! Are you ready? It is time!

These are the days of Elijah!

In verse 30 we find Elijah declaring to the people, "Come near to me!"

The people were tired of the bankrupt answers of the prophets of Baal and they gathered close to Elijah when he called their name. There is a community all around this church waiting on you to call their name. You have completely failed to connect with a community that has become increasingly diverse. You complain about changes in the music... I don't care what it takes...whether it takes Rap, Hip-hop, R&B, Reggae, Alternative music, rappers, drums, Electronica, or whatever...you must be willing to go there. How are you going to call them in if you don't speak their language or play their music? I don't care what it takes...you must find a way to declare to our neighbors..."Rex, come near to us." The people came when Elijah called and our community will too. Are you ready to call so that this community might hear you?

These are the days of Elijah!

Now what did old Elijah do next? He built the altar. Then? He laid the wood. Then? He laid the bull on the altar. Then? Elijah poured water all over it. Verse 33 says he wet that which was supposed to catch on fire. What? Elijah had no doubt that his God would show up and show out.

I want the faith of Elijah. On far too many occasions I have not trusted in God. I have worried if God would show up. Elijah had no doubt...

What would it mean for you to have this much faith in God, Rock Baptist Church? Why don't you stop praying for God to show up and believe that God is not only going to show up but is also going to show out? Wet your altar... Wet the church... Let's prepare ourselves for the fire...

These are the days of Elijah!

In verse 37 Elijah prays:

"Answer me, O LORD, answer me, that this people may know that You, O LORD, are God, and *that* You have turned their heart back again."

Our prayer for Rex, Georgia must be something similar...

God, the father of Abraham, Isaac, Israel, Jesus, and Paul, today let it be known that you alone are God in Rex. We are servants of your holy word God and we sit here awaiting the fire. Answer us, Lord, so that the people of this community might know that you and you alone are God.

Rock Baptist Church, it is time that we cry out with Elijah..."God answer me!" We cry out for ourselves, this church, this community, and this planet. If you cry out...he will answer. Are you ready Rock Baptist Church? Are you ready for the presence of God?

If you are ready, then you, like Elijah, will see the very presence of God...

BOOM!

Verse 38: "Then the fire of the LORD fell and consumed the burnt offering and the wood and the stones and the dust, and licked up the water that was in the trench."

Are you ready?

These are the days of Elijah!

Rock Baptist Church our God is a consuming fire.

We must put our lives on the altar and declare..."God, burn it up!" We must put our materialism, selfishness, hatred, and sexual deviances on the altar and declare..."God burn it up!" It is time for us to give God the Rock Baptist Church. It is time to give God our committees, our deacons, our buildings, our finances and declare..."God burn it up!" You see after the fire is when the true magic begins. When we allow God to consume our lives then we allow God to work. So hurry up! I am ready to see God shock the people of Rex like he did the people of Israel. I want to see the very fire of God. I want to be here when people start running to the doors screaming as the Israelites did in verse 39… "The Lord, He is God!" "The Lord, He is God!" "The Lord, He is God!" I am ready to see the power of God cut loose in Rex, Georgia. I am ready to see the power of God cut loose in all of our lives. I want us all to glow walking out of here today…because we have been in the very presence of God.

These are the days of Elijah!

In verse 40 Elijah explains what to do with the prophets of Baal who had led the nation astray… "Seize the prophets of Baal; do not let one of them escape…slay them!"

If you remain faithful like Elijah, God is going to get the victory here at the Rock Baptist Church and slaughter all of our enemies.

Are you ready?

If we allow God to consume the Rock Baptist Church then we are going to be a part of the eradication of the guns, gangs, perversions, and demons that plague this community. We are going to see God come down and eradicate all that holds us back. This morning may we be the generation who saves this community with the power of God. Bring down the fire, Lord!

The altar will be open for you to claim your part in the coming magic of the fire of the living God.

These are the days of Elijah!

Amen.

10.

By January 2008, I had already spent a year at the Southern Baptist Theological Seminary. This sermon is about doubt. I was honestly just preaching to myself. The truth was that my previous doubts had grown more intense...and I was constantly questioning the love and existence of God. Later, I realized that the intensity arrived when I encountered the rigidity and certainty of the brand of Calvinism or Reformed Theology taught at the Southern Baptist Theological Seminary. In the vestibule, right before I preached this sermon, I broke out in a cold sweat, started hyperventilating, and felt that my chest was about to explode. I didn't know if I was experiencing a panic attack or a heart attack, but I knew it was time to preach.

"Surviving the Storms of Doubt"

New Year's Day Worship

The Rock Baptist Church

January 2008

May the words of my mouth and the meditations of my heart be acceptable in your sight...Oh Lord, be my strength and help me stand.

I have entitled my sermon this morning..."Surviving the Storms of Doubt." But before I begin, I wanted to quickly speak to the pleasure that I take in standing in this pulpit where I have heard the gospel preached and exegeted since my youth. Furthermore, I also wanted to speak to the power and responsibility that I feel in standing here in the gap separating time and eternity to proclaim, "Thus saith the Lord." As I begin in earnest, I want you to ponder what it means to doubt. As I speak to you this morning I want you to recognize that we are all in one of three places at this very moment in time....we are either jut leaving a crisis of doubt, in the midst of a crisis of doubt, or about to head into a crisis of doubt.

Perhaps many of you find those words hard to believe. You are the one who declares like Peter that you will never doubt, question, or deny our Lord. At one point in my life...I was you. Then events transpired that rocked my faith to the very core. The interesting thing is that some of the greatest thinkers and theologians of all time have also experienced this space. The great English Baptist pastor Charles Spurgeon was one such struggler. During the height of his ministry, Spurgeon experienced a depression that slammed him to his knees. Spurgeon often recounted how for three years he did not hear the voice of God or feel his presence and called this time the darkest night of the soul. Spurgeon went on to say that all Christians are going to face similar circumstances and walk through similar darkness.

Spurgeon is a formidable figure in Christian history...but I want to talk to you about a doubter who plays a larger role in the Christian story.

I venture to the time of Jesus. I venture to the man whom Jesus called the greatest man to ever live. A struggler and doubter who almost caved at the time of the greatest crisis he ever faced. I have chosen to focus on the cousin of the one we call the Christ...John the Baptist.

I have divided my sermon into three parts entitled The Revelation, The Crisis, and The Remedy.

The Revelation.

Isaiah 40:3-5 (NASB):

"A voice is calling,

'Clear the way for the LORD in the wilderness;

Make smooth in the desert a highway for our God.'

'Let every valley be lifted up,

And every mountain and hill be made low;

And let the rough ground become a plain,

And the rugged terrain a broad valley;

Then the glory of the LORD will be revealed,

And all flesh will see *it* together;

For the mouth of the LORD has spoken.'"

In this passage we discover the Prophet Isaiah mysteriously speaking of a coming voice in the wilderness that prepares a highway through the desert for the coming messiah. It is interesting that Isaiah uses constructs like the desert and wilderness to describe who this coming voice would be. These constructs are most often used in literature to describe difficult spaces. The prophet would obviously have his ministry in difficult spaces. God granted John the Baptist the permission and peace to use this passage to describe his ministry and himself. John knew that he was preparing the way of God through difficult spaces... This was John's first revelation and affirmation. The second revelation for John the Baptist was delivered through the audible voice of God.

The baptism of Jesus Christ was a mysterious supernatural incredibly human event. The Apostle John takes us to the scene and describes the powerful supernatural ascension of the spirit in great detail in verses 29-34 of his gospel. Matthew further informs us in the third chapter of his gospel that the people actually heard the voice of God.

It is so important to note that John the Baptist actually heard the audible voice of God, interacted with the person of Jesus, and saw the spirit of God descending on

Jesus. Folks, this man got the kind of affirmation that many of us could only dream of. He knew the prophesies. He knew the spirit of God. He knew the audible voice of God. He got to experience all he could have ever dreamed of. Everything was going perfectly according to plan...but then the crisis hit...then the midnight came.

The Crisis

Following Jesus' baptism and the miracles that surrounded the occasion, John the Baptist was put in prison by King Herod. This turn of events was a result of John's public denouncement of Herod's new marriage to his sister-in-law, a flagrant violation of the Hebrew law. As John the Baptist sat cold and shivering in the dungeon, darkness began to overcome his soul. He began to listen to the evil words of the enemy... "If Jesus is the Messiah then why are you stuck here in this dank jail?" "God does not love you." "Jesus is a fake." "A loving God would never put you here." How many of you have found yourself here? How many of you know the struggle of such questions? How we all at one time or another find ourselves in the midnight of sickness, in the midnight of depression, in the midnight of death, or the midnight of loss...the darkness sets in and we begin to succumb to the questions of the enemy. "Why me?" "God, where are you?" "Have you abandoned me, God?"

"Does God even exist at all?" I know these questions well...because they are my questions.

Over the last few months, I have struggled tremendously with the twin darknesses of mania and depression at the Southern Baptist Theological Seminary. I never knew I could be so anxious or depressed. I never knew that such darkness could overcome my life. These struggles are new to me. I have experienced the darkest nights of the soul imaginable. I have asked the dark difficult questions... "Am I here in seminary serving a God that doesn't exist?" "If God loves us then why is there evil?" "Does God care?" I have often come to the conclusion that God doesn't exist...but there is something that keeps me going.

I have been plagued in much the same way that John the Baptist was and I have found inspiration by what happens next. You see John the Baptist sat in prison in the darkness questioning everything he thought he knew. But in the midst of the darkness he knew where to turn for the remedy. He sent his disciples to Jesus.

The Remedy

Matthew 11:2-5 (NASB)

"Now when John, while imprisoned, heard of the works of Christ, he sent *word* by his disciples and said to Him, 'Are You the Expected One, or shall we look for someone else?' Jesus answered and said to them, 'Go and report to John what you hear and see: *the* BLIND RECEIVE SIGHT and *the* lame walk, *the* lepers are cleansed and *the* deaf hear, *the* dead are raised up, and *the* POOR HAVE THE GOSPEL PREACHED TO THEM."

The disciples of John the Baptist went to Jesus and demanded an answer to a basic question... Are you the Messiah or should we look for someone else? Jesus answered powerfully. Do the lame walk? Do the blind see? Do the deaf hear? Are the leapers cured? Are the dead raised? Is God's word preached to the outcasts? Jesus basically stared right back at them and declared... What do you think? Jesus knew John the Baptist had seen and heard about many of the miracles of his ministry. Jesus felt no need to give him a simple yes or no answer...he pointed to the evidence.

When we, like John the Baptist, find ourselves in the dark nights of the soul we must look to the evidence. We look to the evidence of scripture. We look to the evidence of changed lives. We look to the evidence of Christ's presence. We look to the evidence of love. It is imperative that when you doubt God you turn to him as the solution of your struggles. At all times let us remember his promises...

In the darkest of nights when I don't know what to do, I remember the Jesus' sweet words in Matthew 28:20 (NASB), "...lo, I am with you always, even to the end of the age."

When the darkness creeps up let us remember the words of the Psalmist and proclaim on the rooftops, 'When I walk through the valley of the shadow of death...of doubt...of destruction...' No matter how dark. No matter how long. No matter how trying. No matter how intense. I declare that I will fear absolutely positively 'fear no evil for thou art with me.' The remedy of the midnight hour, brothers and sisters, is to remember that dawn is coming and that you never walk alone.

Dawn is coming.... Dawn is coming... Dawn is coming...

If you flip to the back of this book, folks, there is a day coming when there will be no more doubt...a day when we will all return to how we were made...as children of light and love. When you get back there you quickly realize that we win the battle of doubt...in fact, the battle is already being won. There is a day coming and is yet here when the darkness will be quenched with dawn and the trumpets will sound and the dead will rise...and doubt and death shall be no more. Love wins. Jesus wins. On that day...there will be no doubt.

Until that day though, there will be doubt. Some days will be more intense than others...but the remedy is to dive deeper and deeper into the love of God. It is with that love in mind that we leave this place...earnestly believing that He who is in us is much bigger than he who is in the world.

Amen.

11.

I spent the spring of 2008 going from crisis to crisis. My mentor Charles Worthy died, my uncle Donnie Hood shot himself in the heart, and my cousin Jeffrey Hood died in a motorcycle crash. These events set off in my brain the mania component of what I later came to know as Bipolar Disorder. I was truly struggling. I didn't buy the theology of the Southern Baptist Theological Seminary anymore...but I didn't know where to go. I was suicidal. I was losing my mind. I felt my existential reality collapsing. I went backpacking in Europe looking for hope...looking for answers that I felt didn't exist in the spaces I had known. In the old empty cathedrals that dotted the landscape, I decided that I did not want to live without God. When I returned to the United States, I decided to work for the Fountain Anglican Church an Anglican Mission in America church plant in Oxford, Mississippi. During this time, I started to cling to a theology based around a metaphorical return to the paradise of the Garden of Eden in Genesis. I decided that God is presently restoring all things. This theology was far more hopeful for me than the Southern Baptist Theological Seminary theology of Calvinism and Reformed Theology...that God was controlling or destroying all things. My new church was charismatic and taught that the spirit was literally everywhere. It was fun for a little while and then the spirit got greedy. The next two sermons are Garden of Eden and Superman based talks I gave to a youth group I founded called Encounter connected to The Fountain Anglican Church in Oxford, Mississippi.

Superman I

Encounter Youth Group

October 1, 2008

Close your eyes…

Imagine you have on a blue suit with a red cape. You are flying through the air with both fists pressed forward. The world below soars in blurs beneath you. Your face reveals that you have little concern for the cares of this world. Then a voice that has God-like reach declares, "faster than a speeding bullet, more powerful than a locomotive, and able to leap tall buildings in a single bound…he *or she* is Superman *or Superwoman*."

Now open them…

There is a freedom and ease that often comes with having the powers that Superman has. It seems as if his blissful existence is only interrupted when the sins of the world force him into action. Superman enjoys tremendous freedom based on his powers and if sin didn't interrupt his bliss then he would be able to enjoy the freedom of his powers all the time.

Can you imagine a time when all of humanity were Supermen and Superwomen living in perfect bliss without the interruption of sin?

Do you remember Adam and Eve?

In their home...the Garden of Eden...things were very different...

In the Garden, Adam and Eve could run over entire continents and not grow weary.

In the Garden, Adam and Eve could swim around the world.

In the Garden, Adam and Eve could eat anything they wanted and not grow fat.

In the Garden, man had ultimate control over everything on this planet...Adam and Eve could command the lion to play fetch and he would have done it.

In the Garden, there were no funerals because there was no death.

In the Garden, you could literally be run over by a hundred stampeding horses and not be hurt.

In the Garden...we were supermen...we were "faster than a speeding bullet, more powerful than a locomotive, and able to leap tall buildings in a single bound."

In the midst of the Garden, God walked around with Adam and Eve in the cool of the day. Can you imagine going for your daily jog with God? God was physically present.

Then something happened...a mammoth gap between God and man materialized.

Adam and Eve discovered their kryptonite on the Tree of Life. When they disobeyed God's command to not take of the Tree…they traded their freedom for a bite of an apple. Next, came the bondage of sin. Now, we have no ability in and of ourselves to resist sin. Sin is our nature because of Adam's bite. We are prisoners in the dungeon of sin and we are in desperate need of someone to blow open the doors to freedom.

I want to offer you my Superman translation of Lamentations 1:14 (NLT):
God "…wove my sins into chains that imprison me. The Lord took my strength and gave me unto my enemies...my kryptonite. I am helpless in their clutches."

Sin often seems to offer us freedom…unfortunately the freedom to do anything digresses into a slave-like desire to want to do everything. Sin enslaves us turning us into animals and eventually destroying us. We are slaves! What can set us free? Where is our salvation?

Salvation always involves a savior.

Psalm 68:19-20 (NLT):

Praise the Lord! Praise the God our Savior!

For each day he carries us in his arms…

Our God is the God who saves!

God rescues us from death.

Do you want freedom? Do you want to be free? Follow me...

Jesus, the Son of God, became man, was crucified, buried, and resurrected so that we might once more and forever be free. One by one, Jesus is restoring our world and our persons to love. Freedom is trusting that Jesus will complete this process both in ourselves and in the world. Love makes us free.

How do we experience this love? How do we get this salvation?

Jesus says in John 8:31 (NLT):

"You are truly my disciples if you remain faithful to my teachings. And you will know the truth, and the truth will set you free."

So we come...we come to the nail printed hands and feet of Jesus. Trusting in the truth and knowing the love...

Jesus says in Luke 4:18-19 (NLT):

"The Spirit of the Lord is upon me, for he has anointed me to bring Good News to the poor. He has sent me to proclaim that captives will be released, that the blind will see, that the oppressed will be set free, and that the time of the LORD's favor has come. Who wants to see the poor freed, the prisoners freed, the blind freed, the burdened freed, and the battered freed? The time of the Lord's favor has come."

Paul in 2 Corinthians 6:2 (NLT) declares: "Today is the day of salvation!"

For those who already know Jesus, Galations 5:1 (NLT) declares: "Christ has truly set us free. Now make sure that you stay free, and don't get tied up again in slavery to the law."

Are you free? If not...Jesus is always standing beside you with the keys to the prison doors. Let's become supermen again.

Amen.

In the next sermon, I attempted to solidify the students' connection with the person I believe to be the real Superman...Jesus Christ.

Superman II

Encounter Youth Group

October 8, 2008

"Faster than a speeding bullet, more powerful than a locomotive, and able to leap tall buildings in a single bound...he is Superman."

There are numerous times when the plane is going down, the ship is sinking, the train is about to derail, or the car is about to crash and Superman steps in to save those in danger from the catastrophic. This is what Superman is all about...being there when it counts, showing up at the showdown, and making things right. Superman is able to accomplish these things because he is able to do the supernatural the unbelievable.

There is another real figure that has accomplished the supernatural the unbelievable.

Matthew 14:25 (NLT): "About three o'clock in the morning Jesus came toward them, walking on the water."

Mark 6:51 (NLT): Jesus "...climbed into the boat, and the wind stopped. They were totally amazed..."

Matthew 8:27 (NLT): "The disciples were amazed. 'Who is this man?' they asked. 'Even the winds and waves obey him!'"

John 6:21 (NLT): When Jesus stepped into the boat "...immediately they arrived at their destination!"

All of these selections come from the story of Jesus walking on water that appears in the Gospels of Matthew, Mark, and John.

When you encounter a real live Superman...there are always three stages through which you will pass: the preceding events to the encounter, the encounter itself, and the events following the encounter.

In this account, Jesus told the disciples to go on ahead into a crisis. Jesus had the full knowledge that a supernatural occurrence was approaching. The disciples didn't know...but they went anyways. When we follow the commands of Jesus we can expect an encounter with the supernatural.

When Peter is called out of the boat, he joins Jesus in walking on water. When Jesus gets back into the boat, the wind stops. When Jesus gets in the boat, the disciples are transported to their destination. When you have an encounter with the supernatural you experience the supernatural. When you experience Jesus you begin to transcend the boundaries of our present realities to arrive in the otherworldly.

Following these events, the disciples are changed. What type of man is this? Their devotion to the master only grows stronger. The encounter always changes you. One cannot experience Jesus and ever be the same.

Do you want an encounter? Open your hearts and experience the real deal who truly is "Faster than a speeding bullet, more powerful than a locomotive, and able to leap tall buildings in a single bound..." Jesus.

Amen.

12.

In the midst of my time at The Fountain Anglican Church, I was taking twenty-four hours worth of classes at The Southern Baptist Theological Seminary online and by correspondence. I was so ready to get out of the school and be finished with my degree. One of the classes I was taking was a preaching class. The professor expected all students to preach one expository sermon and videotape it. The following is that sermon.

There were multiple other factors occurring at the same time as this sermon. Due to many circumstances, some personal and some theological, I was ready to dissolve my relationship with the frighteningly charismatic lead priest at the church. This served as a primary point of distraction. I also worried about the sermon because I knew that my theology, although still moderately conservative, was nowhere close to the fundamentalist Southern Baptist Theological Seminary theology anymore. Lastly, at the last minute, one of the associate priests at St. Peter's Episcopal Church, the church that our little church broke away from, showed up to scope out the church. She sneered at me the entire time I was preaching. In spite of all of this, I think I did pretty well. This would be the last time I spoke at The Fountain Anglican Church.

The Fountain Anglican Church

Oxford, Mississippi

October 14, 2008

True Religion: To Live As If It Really Matters

James 1:26-27 (NASB):

If anyone thinks himself to be religious, and yet does not bridle his tongue but deceives his *own* heart, this man's religion is worthless. Pure and undefiled religion in the sight of *our* God and Father is this: to visit orphans and widows in their distress, *and* to keep oneself unstained by the world.

There are three parts to my talk this evening:

The Nature of False Religion

The Practical Outworking of True Religion

The Practical Inworking of True Religion

The Nature of False Religion

We are a people who thrive on being religious. We go through the rituals, we sing the songs, we speak highly of Jesus, and we often do good things. We put Jesus on our cars and around our necks. We listen to the right music. We hang out with the right people. We read the right books. We are so religious.

James tells us that religion is the problem.

Our language and practices often deceive us into thinking that we are right with God. We deceive our own hearts and often our friends don't help too much. They say things like... "Well you have taught Sunday School for 40 years!" "You are at the church all the time!" "You proclaim Jesus everyday with your necklace." Religion is incredibly self-deceptive and incredibly destructive. Communion with Jesus is based on relationship. You see, participating in the right activities and saying the right things are nothing more than hot air unless one's heart rests firmly in a relationship with Jesus. Without that relationship life is worthless and meaningless.

There are many false religious teachers and prophets out there prowling around and leading people astray. Joel Osteen's preaching of a false gospel of positivity comes to mind. False religion is to believe or teach that you can do anything productive or good apart from the love and relationship of Jesus Christ. To live as if it is all about your best life now is to live as if others don't matter. James begs us to live differently.

We exist as a church and as Christians to proclaim that Jesus is The Way, The Truth, and The Life! There is no path through our individual selves. Please understand that if your goal is your best life now apart from Jesus then you will have hell to pay later. We must connect to Jesus.

Jesus is true religion.

The Practical Outworking of True Religion

Our desire is a religion of love that matters. Love comes from relationship. Jesus says in Matthew 22:37-39 (NASB): "'You shall love the Lord your God with all your heart, and with all your soul, and with all your mind.' This is the great and foremost commandment. The second is like it, 'You shall love your neighbor as yourself.'" Jesus says that loving God and loving each other are closely related. In John 13:35 (NASB) Jesus said, "By this all men will know that you are My disciples, if you have love for one another." The consequence of not having the love of Jesus in your heart or loving each other is hell pure and simple. The root of Jesus is the root of love and we must have Jesus in order to have love for others. James gives us two examples of the outworking of true religion: visiting orphans and widows in their distress. This example is very important.

During New Testament times, the orphan and the widow were seen as the most helpless persons in society. James is telling us that binding ourselves to the least in society is the practical outworking of having the true religion of Jesus Christ. This is a fascinating component of this passage. According to James, the outworking of true religion is not church service, church activities, church discussions, church singing, church ritual, or church ceremonies. The truth of the matter is that true religion has nothing to do with the church unless the church is concerned with what is going on out there with those who need us the most. We have to get out of this building and into the world of the least. That is where Jesus would be. Love will meet us out there.

The Practical Inworking of True Religion

Jesus, while he was here walking, living, and breathing on this planet, maintained righteousness and kept himself unstained by the world through maintaining his prayer life and walking in relationship with his father. Why do we so often think that we are different? Those who fall to the temptations of sin and unrighteousness are not walking with Jesus. There must be an intentionality to pray and walk with Jesus if one is to remain unstained by this world. Jesus taught us that righteousness is important.

Do you want to keep yourself unstained by the world? Then first consider the things that are important to you. If they do not have to do with love of God and neighbor then your affinities are misplaced. The practical inworking of true religion is a willingness to purify one's self in order to more intimately connect with Jesus. We leave the things of this world behind so that we might know Jesus as we have been fully known.

In closing, I would like to read to you the words of James 1:26-27 from The Message: "Anyone who sets himself up as 'religious' by talking a good game is self-deceived. This kind of religion is hot air and only hot air. Real religion, the kind that passes muster before God the Father, is this: Reach out to the homeless and loveless in their plight, and guard against corruption from the godless world."

Do you have true religion? Prove it!

Amen.

13.

It meant so much at this time for me to be asked to preach at The Rock Baptist Church. I left The Fountain Anglican Church a few months prior to this service...due to multiple moral failings on the part of the frighteningly charismatic lead priest...and really felt low. This sermon continues to speak of Eden with an idea that a restoration is both present and approaching. Having also finished classes at The Southern Baptist Theological Seminary, I felt freer in my theology. This was the first sermon that I let my increasingly progressive feelings about queer persons come out. For many, the sentence referencing queer persons might not sound progressive...but for my home church and me they were a radical departure from the hateful statements we had grown accustomed to.

January 1, 2009

New Year's Day Worship

The Rock Baptist Church

We Were Meant to Live for So Much More: A Theology of Eden

A few words from John Milton's *Paradise Lost*:

Of man's first disobedience, and the fruit

Of that forbidden tree, whose mortal taste
Brought death into the world, and all our woe,
With the loss of Eden, we lost everything.

This morning I stand to declare a need to start this 2009 by looking to our beginnings. For it is way back in Eden that we find the fullness of ourselves. My how we have traveled since the day that mortal sin took place. As I stop to look around our world today, I see the realization of Matthew 24. I see wars and rumors of wars. I see nation rising against nation and kingdom against kingdom. I see people killing each other. Molestations and murder fill the news. My God...how far we have traveled from that land known as Eden. The name of God is hot on our lips but cold in our hearts. I yearn for Eden.

When I think about how long ago it was and how far we have traveled from Eden...I feel the pain of Jeremiah 9:1 (NLT):

If only my head were a pool of water and my eyes a fountain of tears, I would weep day and night for all my people who have been slaughtered.

Do you remember, beloved, that time in which there was no pain, no death, no hunger, and no violence?

Do you remember, beloved, when people truly loved each other and walked with God in the cool of the day?

You might say I'm crazy...but I remember.

In my heart of hearts...I remember.

I yearned for Eden this past year.

I sat next to my dear friend and mentor Charles Worthy as he died of lung cancer. I loved Charles so much and miss him terribly. I often wonder how I am going to push through ministry without him. I listened to him take some of his last gasps of air. He is gone. The loss seems eternal.

I yearned for Eden this past year.

Last spring, I received a phone call from my dad. As his voice quivered...he asked me to go and tell my grandparents that my Uncle Donnie Hood had shot himself. I traveled to their home and stammered out the news. I cried. They lost it. We were forced to take my grandmother to the emergency room. She was fine. We experienced his funeral over the next few days. He is gone. The loss seems eternal.

I yearned for Eden this past year.

In late spring, my cousin Jeffrey Hood died in a motorcycle crash. He had just lost his dad and now he was joining him. His struggles often disrupted his relationships with our family. I wish that I had known him better. He is gone. The loss seems eternal.

I yearned for Eden this past year.

There were wars worldwide. Many of which the United States instigated and perpetuated. Many families received news that their loved ones would not be coming home. Think about living in Baghdad as bombs consistently exploded outside of your house.

I yearned for Eden this past year.

The rich continue to get richer and the poor continue to get poorer.

I yearned for Eden this past year.

Even as I speak, my Aunt Dianne Wallace lies dying of bone cancer in Snellville, Georgia.

What in the hell is going on?

Oh, how I yearn for Eden!

The confluence of evil consistently causes me to cry out to God with the knowledge that something was tragically awry and wrong. These tragedies caused me to search deep in my heart and long for a day in which none of this would have ever happened. I have hope today not because of what is but rather because of what was. Is it possible to turn back the clock?

I believe that every human heart has the ability to remember what it was like there in Eden. The longing for justice and righteousness to roll down like a mighty stream is a remembrance. The desire to know and walk with God is a remembrance. The seething anger at the injustice of sickness and death is a remembrance. In these remembrances we find the answer and the way forward.

When Jesus came to earth, lived, died, and arose...he took us back to Eden. Jesus reverses the curse of death. Jesus tells us that it is possible to be fully alive once more. Jesus is the avenue back to Eden. The Apostle Paul tells us in his second letter to the church at Corinth that even now God through Jesus is reconciling the entire world. Connect to Jesus and you begin your individual journey back to Eden.

Those individuals who have chosen to follow Jesus also have been given a responsibility to lead the world back...back to Eden...to set the world back to love and back to right. Eden is not just a call to connect with Jesus, but also a call to connect the world to Jesus. It is time that we reverse the curse and take back our world for the Kingdom of the Living God. We stand with Jesus in resistance to a world gone mad. We truly are the resistance!

Each time you put love in the hearts of the hurting...

You are the resistance!

Each time you put food in the mouths of the hungry...

You are the resistance!

Each time you fight for justice and equality...

You are the resistance!

Each time you fight for peace in a world ravaged by war...

You are the resistance!

Each time you preach the Gospel to a world devoid of hope and love...

You are the resistance!

We are the resistance!

When you act in resistance you send forth tiny rays of hope that combine with the rays of hope created by others to create an overwhelming array of light which can sweep down the mightiest walls of oppression and darkness.

This morning in the spirit of Eden...beloved I must declare to you that...

I am against violence and war in all shapes and sizes because I do not believe that shed blood can bring about peace.

I am against our economic systems because they take from the poor to shore up the bank accounts of the rich.

I am against oppression in all its nasty forms because we serve a God who has come to set the captives free.

I am against hate because we serve a God that has called us to love our enemies as ourselves.

If you are going to be a part of the resistance then your thinking is going to have to change. The old forms are not going to work anymore. We represent Jesus and our minds must transcend the narrow categories we are often given here in this society.

We are the church. We are the only hope that the world has. The resistance has already begun. Our part begins now.

We desire an end to hunger so we are going to start feeding people in this community.
We desire to end the cycle of poverty so we are going to work so that Clayton County schools will be the best and most equitable in the world.
We want an end to hate so we are going to start loving each other.
We want to end racism so we are going to start interacting with others based on the content of their character and not the color of their skin.
We desire an end to homophobia so we are going to start loving homosexuals.
We hunger for world evangelization so we are going to walk across the street to tell our neighbor about Jesus.

The world needs us. Beloved this is our time. The Kingdom of God is breaking in...through us into the world. Let's go back to Eden. Will you join me?

Amen.

14.

Running out of options, I decided to work again at a familiar place...Wadley Baptist Church. I knew it was going to be conservative, but I needed a job. I guess I thought I was going to soften their hard theologies. This sermon was a response to the financial collapse that had just occurred in the nation. My Jesus-inspired progressive economic values are on full display.

Sunday Worship

Wadley Baptist Church

July 2, 2009

Our Economy and God

Today is a day of tremendous crisis. This day we find ourselves in the midst of great economic turmoil. We all find ourselves groping around seeking where to go...such economic times produce drastic circumstances through which people are forced to maintain life. In Detroit, 18% of the population is currently unemployed. Rates are not much better elsewhere. Nationwide, 86 million people live without health insurance or close to one out of three people in our country. When these people get sick where do they go? Who is there to help them? Crime rates have skyrocketed across the planet as people grow more and more desperate. Home break-ins, robberies, and other kinds of theft are happening all over. Just last week a man was killed for $20. $20? In this area, factories are closing and jobs are being lost at a much higher rate than factories are opening or jobs are being brought in. Plantation Patterns gone... Wellborn Cabinets claims to be in tremendous economic distress... The times are undoubtedly difficult and demand critical reflection. How are we to respond as Christians? How are we to be Christ in a world that has gone economically mad?

I speak to you the words of Jesus from Matthew's Gospel chapter 25 verses 41 to 45 (The Message):

"Then he will turn to the 'goats,' the ones on his left, and say, 'Get out, worthless goats! You're good for nothing but the fires of hell. And why? Because...

I was hungry and you gave me no meal,

I was thirsty and you gave me no drink,

I was homeless and you gave me no bed,

I was shivering and you gave me no clothes,

Sick and in prison, and you never visited.'"

"Then those 'goats' are going to say, 'Master, what are you talking about? When did we ever see you hungry or thirsty or homeless or shivering or sick or in prison and didn't help?'"

"Jesus will answer them, 'I'm telling the solemn truth: Whenever you failed to do one of these things to someone who was being overlooked or ignored, that was me...you failed to do it to me.'"

Do you hear those words of Jesus? Let them ring in your ears and challenge your soul. Indeed in this very community, people have lost their jobs and have no work. Indeed in this very community, people are lonely and without support. Indeed in this very community, people are on the brink of foreclosure and have nowhere else to go. Indeed in this very community, there are people who are homeless and in need of help. Indeed in this very community, there are people thirsty and people starving. Indeed in this very community, there are people lonely and imprisoned. Do not be fooled by the ambiance of affluence...there are people in this very community who are living in shacks with no running water or electricity. I have seen them. I have met them. Jesus said, what you have done to all of these people you have done to me. Jesus then is running around everywhere else in this community except this church. What are you doing to Jesus, Wadley Baptist Church? In the name of Jesus, I demand an answer.

Since most of you are struggling to formulate an answer. Let me help you... I have heard the ways that you speak to each other. You are telling your friends not to go over to his side of town. You turn your nose up at him when he crosses the street. You believe that you are better than he is. You tell your kids that they better not hang out with him and if they date him that you will kill him. You let him starve by denying him the excess food from your tables. Simply throwing it in the trash. You let him go naked by hording the excess clothes you never wear. You have called him nigger, spic, faggot, trash, and a whole host of other names. These are your typical interactions with Jesus in Wadley, Alabama. In your arrogance and abundance you are denying the very God you claim to worship. What is going on? Where are our hearts?

Wadley United Methodist Church right across the parking lot from our church has a normal attendance of about 15 to 20 in comparison to our 100. Despite their paltry attendance, they feed a good deal of the poor people that you seemed to have forgotten with their feeding ministry. How do you respond??? You respond by leaning out the windows of your cars looking to see who should and shouldn't be there getting food. In the midst of the greatest economic downturn since the Great Depression, not only are you lacking in your provision of help...you actually have the nerve to criticize those who are seeking help. Shame on you! Wadley United Methodist Church has been seeking to progress the Lord's Acre concept to provide people with food from the extra crops harvested in this area. How do you respond? You declare, 'If they don't work then they shouldn't eat!' I am glad that Jesus Christ does not play by your rules. If you don't behave right then no grace. Can you imagine where we would all be with your rules? I've got it...we would all be burning in hell. What are you doing to Jesus folks? Where is your love?

Loving the least is something that we are commanded to be a part of. As Christians, we are measured based on our love for the least. Is Jesus in you? The answer to that question lies in how you treat the least. Wadley Baptist Church we must wake up this morning to the voice of Jesus Christ. We must begin to help those who are living in this community who need our help. We must reach out to those who are sitting in this congregation that need our help.

I know that many of you sitting in this room are struggling and fall under the category of the least. I encourage you based on the words of Jesus in Matthew 4:4 (NASB), "'Man shall not live on bread alone, but on every word that proceeds out of the mouth of God.'" Know that God is incarnated into your struggle and with you. I also encourage you to seek help from those in this room. If the people of this church don't help you then go to another church where both Jesus and love are actually present.

In this great recession, is Wadley Baptist Church going to be greedy or Jesus?

Now, in the name of Jesus, I command you to do that which is right. Go feed the hungry. Go clothe the naked. Go sit with the lonely. Go get acquainted with the prisoners. Go love. Go be Jesus Christ.

Amen.

15.

This sermon is a response to a multiplicity of things. Throughout my tenure at Wadley Baptist Church, I had grown tired of their closed, clean, legalistic God. Jesus was always all about rules and looked just like them. I think for many people, I didn't look like their Jesus. I felt that behind every smile there existed deep skepticism of my prophetic spirit. This sermon is a response to all of the superficial cleanliness I experienced. The week before I gave this sermon, I was assaulted and threatened on a small country road while out on a run. The custodian, who also had responsibility over the sound system, had grown tired of my youth group cranking up the music in the church. His response was to grab me and threaten to kill me. Everyone in the church knew about the incident and I felt the need to be prophetic. I also served under a pastor who was very clean, yet failed to do the right thing when this situation happened. I wanted the church to know that clean appearances are not more important than people or God.

Wadley Baptist Church

Sunday Morning Worship

September 5, 2009

Cleanliness is Not Next to Godliness...

I must begin by giving credit and thanks to my advisor and the Charles Howard Candler Professor of American Church History at Emory University's Candler School of Theology, E. Brooks Holifield, for delivering a recent sermon that ignited my interest in this particular text and supplied some of the content I use today.

There is a grave danger facing Wadley Baptist Church today. It is a pervading stifling spirit of legalism that assumes that right practice is equal to right belief. We govern our lives and the lives of others by the old moral mandate that "cleanliness is next to Godliness..." You have such a concern for cleanliness. Your discussions are filled with how so and so is acting or what so and so is doing. You have more concern for the outer individual than you do the inner individual. This does not sound like the spirit of Jesus to me.

It is interesting that when we read the gospel accounts of the life of Christ, most stories and instances portray a Christ who does not seem to care about the acts of the perpetrator...but rather seems only concerned about the healing of the perpetrator's soul. Just last week, Wadley Methodist Pastor Sherrill preached on Jesus' interactions with the woman he met at the well. Did the Lord give her instructions on what to do about her man issues? Did the Lord resort to the tactics of the disciples and talk about her? OR Did the Lord offer her the living water that she needed to be made whole? Likewise, when Jesus approaches the woman caught in adultery that is about to be stoned by the Pharisees does he say... What have you done, you nasty promiscuous woman? Who have you been running around with? NO! Jesus says, "Do these men still condemn you? Nor do I...Go and sin no more." In Matthew 15, we find the disciples being lambasted by the Pharisees because they have not been washing their hands in accordance with Jewish law. Just to make sure there is no doubt, Jesus existed in a time that had laws for everything. In response to the Pharisees' hand washing criticisms, Jesus does not say...Ok boys, go wash up and come back to dinner. OR Repent for not washing and then you can eat. Jesus responds in Matthew 15:11 (NLT), "It's not what goes into your mouth that defiles you; you are defiled by the words that come out of your mouth." It is the inside of the human that Jesus is concerned about. In each of these instances we discover the very heart of a loving God. Jesus is a God crying out not for more of our rules but rather for more of our hearts. Cleanliness is not next to Godliness.

We have got to stop confusing matters of practice with the internal matters of the heart. The difference of which we speak is the difference between the shallow and the deep. Are we more concerned about hands than hearts? We must stop letting our desire for laws and right answers betray us. Some of you might legalistically not drink a lick of alcohol yet you cannot remember the last time you shared the love of Jesus with someone. There is not one verse in all the scriptures that prohibits alcohol consumption but we are explicitly told to "Go to the nations..." At this church we take great pride in our sound system...even to the point that we are willing to get violent over it...but how is it helping our outreach for the Kingdom of

God? We are so proud of our new toilets...yet when was the last time they put food in the mouths of the hungry? We are washing our hands and not purifying our hearts. Jesus is looking at us today and begging us to let go of our silly rules that take away from our ministry to the hearts of others. Where are your hearts...with rules or Jesus? Cleanliness is not next to Godliness.

Jesus Christ is the God slayer. Following Jesus should cleanse us of all loyalties apart from him (that includes toilets, rules, carpets, standards, and sound systems). The danger of legalism is that it creates a God around the idea that we can save ourselves. We cannot. Salvation comes through Jesus alone. This morning may we leave this place remembering that cleanliness is not next to Godliness...and put Christ back on the throne of our hearts where he belongs.

Amen.

Source:

E. Brooks Holifield. Sermon Preached on 26 August 2009 at Emory University's Cannon Chapel. https://itunes.apple.com/itunes-u/cannon-chapel-sermons-cannon/id422868582?mt=10.

16.

I had just started working on a Master of Theology at Emory University when I began to engage Emory Intervarsity Christian Fellowship. I felt that a sermon in front of one of the larger evangelical groups on campus would be a good time to distance myself from the word "saved." I had grown so tired of the word and wanted to challenge the group to imagine new salvation language. I think I was already on my way out of the fundamentalist evangelical context...but this sermon solidified my exit in my mind and in the minds of those who heard me.

Emory University Intervarsity Christian Fellowship

Weekly Meeting

October 15, 2009

"The Grave Danger of Being Saved"

Christianity is always contextual. We always interact with Christ and experience God from our individual contexts. So initially, I need to tell you about myself. I am Jeff Hood. I grew up in a Southern Baptist, largely evangelical context. I hold a

Masters of Divinity from an evangelical seminary, The Southern Baptist Theological Seminary in Louisville, Kentucky. I was ordained into the ministry by an evangelical Southern Baptist church. I speak to you tonight as an evangelical.

Throughout my upbringing, our church consistently spoke of the need to be "saved." Every sermon that was preached had one primary goal...to get you down the aisle. The reason that was supposed to always get you out of your seat was the threat of hell. Fear became something I knew quite well. About this time each year, our church would take all of the youth to an event called the Tribulation Trail. The idea was to take you through the Book of Revelation and what would happen to you if you got left behind. I think all of you know this type of language. Each year the church putting on the Tribulation Trail proclaimed glory to God for the thousands of people who made professions of faith. I myself remember getting "saved" somewhere around 36 times when I was growing up...with many of these instances occurring scared stiff on the Tribulation Trail. The problem then and the problem now is that evangelical discussions of hell, raptures, and being left behind created and create a salvation culture based on fear. The word "saved" fits right in with this fear driven Christianity.

What comes to your mind when you ponder the word "saved?" I often think about drowning and needing someone to throw me a life raft. After the life raft has been thrown and I am out of the water, I have been "saved." The word becomes less and less useful except to describe one moment in time that I experienced. The story represents the difficulties we create when we consistently use the word "saved" to describe someone coming to know the Lord. "Saved" points to one event that saves you from eminent danger. This makes it seem that salvation is only about being saved from hell. "Saved" also describes one moment in time and ultimately fails to describe a lifetime of relationship. "Saved" promotes a lie that if we say a prayer then we know Jesus. Ultimately, "saved" is a selfish word that describes our desire to save ourselves rather than our desire to know Jesus. The Christian is primarily seeking to become like Jesus not to be "saved" from hell. Our idolization of this word "saved" has got to stop. The word "saved" has not served us well and will not serve us well in the future. We must revolutionize our thinking and language to reflect the words of Jesus.

In Luke 18 (NIV), Jesus meets the questioning rich young ruler...

"Good teacher, what must I do to inherit eternal life?"

"You know the commandments..."

"All these I have kept since I was a boy..."

"You still lack one thing. Sell everything you have and give to the poor and you will have treasure in heaven. Then come, follow me."

"When he heard this, he became very sad, because he was a man of great wealth."

Often when we talk about faith, love, and salvation we rarely turn to Luke 18. There are other places that are more prominent and perhaps more comfortable. John 3:16 (NIV), "For God so loved the world that he gave his one and only Son, that whoever believes in him shall not perish but have eternal life." Romans 8:38-39 (NIV), "For I am convinced that neither death nor life, neither angels nor demons, neither the present nor the future, nor any powers, neither height nor depth, nor anything else in all creation, will be able to separate us from the love of God that is in Christ Jesus our Lord." Jeremiah 1:5 (NIV), "Before I formed you in the womb I knew you, before you were born I set you apart..." These verses of adoption, grace, mercy, hope, and love are used all the time to talk about following Jesus...but why not Luke 18? I tend to think it has to do with the fact that the verses demand so much...everything. I think most modern evangelicals are like the rich young ruler and want to follow Jesus...but ultimately they don't want to sacrifice themselves in the process. Do you want to be "saved" or do you want to give Jesus everything?

Now is the time to forget being "saved" as we begin to learn about what it means to truly follow Jesus. I think Luke 18 is a good place to start. How often do we pray Lord I will go where you go, do what you do, and be what you are? How often do we pray that prayer and realize we are asking for death? How often do we pray that prayer with the thought that we need to sell everything we have and follow Jesus? The question of Luke 18 is not whether you want to get "saved" or not...but rather whether you are ready to go all the way. Perhaps the grave danger in getting "saved" is missing the boat and thinking that praying a prayer is enough for a life with Christ. When a teaching distracts or leads us away from the message of Jesus, it is by definition heresy. Then the word "saved" is heretical. Salvation is a lifestyle and not a moment. Salvation is not a past event but rather a present reality. Jesus said that today is the day of salvation. Jesus is asking you to give it all. Will you trust in the "saved" lingo or follow Jesus? I chose Jesus.

Amen.

17.

This sermon represents my attempt at the Inaugural Festival of Young Preachers to be an apologist against and a prophet to the evangelical community. I preached it in the middle of my academic career at Emory University. The point was to make a statement. I wanted the people sitting in that room to know that the evangelical community had been and was presently wrong in their dealings with the greatest moral issues of our time and in need of a radical reformation. I made my point. I grew more inclusive and compassionate at Emory. I have no question that this sermon reflects the very different evangelical that I had become.

January 8, 2010

*This sermon was first published in *A Beautiful Thing: Sermons from the Festival of Young Preachers* (Chalice Press).

The Danger of Selfish Piety: An Apology and Promise on Behalf of the Evangelical Community

The Rev. Jeffrey K. Hood Jr.

MDiv, The Southern Baptist Theological Seminary

ThM (Cand.), Emory University

Brothers and Sisters, this afternoon we gather in the midst of great turmoil. We are a people bewildered and afraid. We look around and see nothing but tragedy.

Wars rage on every horizon. The United States being currently involved in conflicts in Iraq and Afghanistan...regularly killing and regularly being killed. Pain is inflicted on the families of those who hold the guns and on those being senselessly massacred in the name of an elusive peace. Economic recession has broken our stride. People all over the world are being tossed out of their homes as greedy banks foreclose on their homes, and these are the lucky ones. Many never had a house to start with. Millions of people all over the world live without the essential means to survive. This phenomenon is usually coupled with no hope of securing such means. Violence in many different forms rule over our lands and evil rules in the hearts of men...and yet, brothers and sisters, still we gather...here at the Inaugural Festival of Young Preachers, to celebrate an art form that seeks to give people the great weapons of truth and hope to rise above such madness and seek a newer world.

Indeed it is in this spirit of a newer world that I approach an event that is the greatest climax in all of human history…The Resurrection of Jesus Christ…seeking to rise above the aforementioned madness and folly.

The Christian community has always looked to the empty tomb for direction in the midst of great peril. Today is no different. We look to that tomb because it is at the center of all that we know.

Yet today I arise not unfamiliar with the previous Friday. This day was a day of intense desolation and destruction. It was a time in which the very Son of God cried out, "My God, My God why have you forsaken me…" (Matthew 27:46 NIV). Disciples ran in every direction not sure how to continue on. There was a spirit of defeat amongst the followers of Jesus Christ. Today we sit here aware that such defeat would not last for long.

This was an important day and we must never forget that this was the day that the atonement for the sins of man was secured.

But, brothers and sisters, we must also not forget that ours is a tale of two days. Far too often we speak of the atonement and we fail to speak of the restoration that is the resurrection.

I am very familiar with this phenomenon. I was raised like any good modern evangelical to be a Good Friday Christian. I was taught to stay there at the cross on Friday, mining the nether regions of my soul. I was taught to follow the rules or the aforementioned atonement would not be for me. I was taught, "to know that I know that I know that I know" that I truly believed that Jesus died for my sins. There has been a common thread for me contained in everything I have been taught as an evangelical from the youth group I grew up in to the highest reaches of evangelical education. Indeed, like any other modern evangelical, I was taught that Christianity was all about me. Brothers and Sisters, there is grave danger in only being a Good Friday Christian.

When one is taught only to be a Good Friday Christian he is unfortunately not educated as to the restoration that accompanies the resurrection of Jesus Christ. In the resurrection there is a conquering of death that is complete. In the resurrection there is conquering of all that holds us down in torment here on this earth. In the resurrection there is a promise of a new world that we have a duty to work for. In the resurrection there is an end to all that afflicts us and yet mine is a community that has completely failed to be a resurrection and, in turn, a restoration people.

The evangelical community has neglected the greatest social, moral, and political issues of our time as we all huddle around the cross participating in a selfish piety that does not give a damn about the restoration of a planet. I have cried many a night when I hear my people screaming about political issues drowning out the cries of the hungry in our streets. I have wept over the fact that the evangelical community is more concerned with "knowing that we know that we know that we know" to the neglect of healing a broken world. A resurrection and restoration people do not live like this. Indeed a restoration people should care more about others than they do about their own power and influence.

And so on this day, I arise to apologize for my people...the evangelical community. We have been seduced by our own piety. We have been seduced by our newfound power and influence. We have been seduced by our leaders to place ourselves far before anyone else. We have not cared at all about deep injustices that are taking place all over the world and for that we are deeply sorry.

Today, I bring this confession on behalf of a new generation of evangelicals that is absolutely fed up with the selfishness of a communion that has failed to be a resurrection and restoration people. We have often proven through our actions that we would just as soon leave humanity dead in the grave of sin and destruction than take any focus off of our own piety and power. Ours is a communion that has spoken often of a Jesus that is mine, but failed miserably in speaking of a God that absolutely loves the world and wants to see it put to right. We have cheered on blatant sins...whether that be in the form of war, racism, poverty, healthcare, or immigration...as we in the very same breath call it God's will.

It is a stinging indictment that the evangelical community is known for everything it is against and very little for what it is for. We have placed our political candidates before you long before we ever get around to placing our Savior in your midst. Indeed, Jesus seems quite often to be noticeably absent from most of our efforts. We have so often kept our views fresh on our lips while God and God's people are far from our hearts. And in this, our selfishness, we have failed billions.

The evangelical church I spent much time in as a child and many churches just like it represent our community and this phenomenon of selfish piety very well. The church was a church that found itself in an increasingly uncomfortable situation in the community. Everyone in the church was upper middle class and everyone outside the church was dying in his or her respective fight against the various systems of oppression that fill our lands. Crime and creeping poverty surrounded the church on all sides. During worship services it was absolutely impossible not to hear the sounds of gunshots and sirens as the pianist and organist played. After some time, the people realized that the church could not just sit there and do nothing any longer. They decided to act swiftly. And act they did... The next business meeting the church decided on a unanimous vote that the church should move to the suburbs. Jesus said that we would find him amongst the least of these. Well, at this church, and in many evangelical churches just like it, when Jesus moved in to the neighborhood the church quickly moved out.

Our generation of evangelicals seeks churches that change the world. Not churches that leave when the world changes.

Today, I confess our actions on behalf of the evangelical community. Jesus, we have failed you and your people, over and over and over again. We confess our sin and seek redemption knowing that you rose from the dead to convert us not from life to something more than life but from something less than life to the reality of a world made fully alive.

Brothers and sisters of the broader Christian world we, like you, seek the promise of the restoration and we seek it, not just for ourselves, but also for the entire world. The death and resurrection of Jesus Christ represent a demand as well as a promise; the demand is that we bind ourselves to the crucified Christ and the promise is that through pledging our loyalty to the risen Christ we will bring about a new world. This means that all loyalties to systems and institutions of injustice that perpetuate the destruction of this world must cease.

Today, brothers and sisters, we declare that we will be loyal to such systems and institutions no more. We seek to join the broader Christian community in seeking the new world promise of the resurrection. We stand united with you...

We stand united with you against the destruction of life.

We stand united with you against war and violence.

We stand united with you against systems of economic oppression that rule our lands.

We stand united with you against the evils of prejudice and racism in all forms.

We hurt. We are filled with pain. We long to see this new world promise of the resurrection.

We stand united with you against all forms of oppression and injustice so that we will no longer be part of the problem but part of the solution.

We promise to never turn our backs on God's people again.

This day we stand with you...

We stand united with you to clear a way for the Lord in the wilderness: to make smooth a highway for our God. That every valley may be lifted up, and every mountain and hill be made low; that the rough ground will become a plain and that the rugged terrain be made a broad valley.

We believe with you that then, and only then, will the glory of the Lord be revealed, and all flesh will be able to see it together crying out in one joyous accord:

O death, where is thy sting?

O grave, where is thy victory? *

Can it begin today brother and sisters? Can such unity begin today? Will this be the day that we Christians finally begin to seek a new world together? I am tired of this dark tomb...

Amen.

*(Isaiah 40:3-5/1 Corinthians 15:54-55 NASB)

18.

I was asked by a moderate Baptist publication in Georgia to write an article explaining why I believe 20s and 30s were leaving the church...this is the article I created. It got rejected and never appeared in print. I have had a love hate relationship with moderate Baptists ever since. Constructing this article also helped me to realize that I am not moderate anything.

Why the 20s and 30s are leaving the church...

February 24, 2010

"But if you will not listen to it, My soul will sob in secret for such pride; And my eyes will bitterly weep And flow down with tears, Because the flock of the LORD has been taken captive." (Jer. 13:17 NASB)

Brothers and Sisters, we are a people overly confident and blissfully distracted. Yet we have no peace within: we invest ourselves in endless infighting, petty bickering, and merciless judgmentalism. And yet our churches are shrinking... Young people are hemorrhaging from our pews in astounding numbers. Wonder why? I look around and see nothing but the tragedy of certainty.

Our churches peddle certainty like a drug. We have assured people that we have the answers and used these assumptions to construct litmus tests for salvation. I am very aware of the dangers of such tests...my own evangelical tradition has been quick to exclude anyone who disagrees with their often narrow understandings of orthodoxy. Now, I look around and see no one left to challenge such assumed certainty. In the midst of such purging, our hearts have grown cold towards our neighbors and to the groans of our ailing planet.

My mainline brothers and sisters have not escaped this phenomenon either. The only difference is their exchange of orthodoxy for a secular and modernistic thought that is just as narrow in its demands. They have banished all who disagree from their midst terming them "backwards," "sexist," "racist"—or perhaps even worse—"conservative." In their churches, I sought refuge from the sting of a narrow fundamentalism, only to find a secular orthodoxy that is no less strident in its excessive stipulations on my thinking. They champion a love of neighbor yet their love does not extend to their more conservative neighbors who have either purged them or left their denominations. The body of Christ has been broken, dear brothers and sisters, but not in fellowship.

Make no mistake; all sides have their own agendas and most point away from Christ towards a greater power in this present age. The certainty of your generation is blatant and speaks quite loudly of what your chief concerns entail. God is not mocked and nor are we.

Young people are not fooled by such charades. Your generation has denied us a place to ask our questions and so we remain silent. Your generation has denied us community so we stay at home. Your generation has denied us a place to be active in the genuine restoration of the planet and so we wait. In the midst of your certainty you have denied us the church and the love of Jesus Christ.

Your generation's various purging and demands have been quite effective don't you think...

On your watch, the church has been seduced by power, and has lost its way. Your generation has claimed to be a people of peace yet wars rage on every horizon with your blessing. Your generation has claimed to care so much about life yet premature death occurs daily for many throughout the world due to perpetual greed. Your generation loves to speak of hope yet you have so often completely dashed all of ours.

We cannot hear Jesus over your continual shouts at one another.

Perhaps it is time that your generation show us exactly who Jesus Christ is by loving like Him and tearing down these hardened walls of assumptions. It is indeed past time that we become known, not for our agendas, but for our love. We cannot wait a single second, for the future of the church, hear our cries...

I pray yours is not the generation forced to turn out the lights of our sanctuaries for the final time.

19.

I was proud when my father was elected Clayton County Fire and EMS Chief and Director of the Clayton County Emergency Management Agency. I was even prouder when he asked me to pray at his inauguration. This is a prayer for my father and for all of those who were going to come in contact with him.

Inauguration of Fire Chief Jeff Hood, Sr.

Clayton County Government Building

112 Smith Street, Jonesboro, Georgia

April 21, 2011

Prayer

God of all comfort, through whom we live, breathe, and have our being, thank you for meeting us here.

In these difficult days of financial instability and global insurrection…we ask that even in this time of celebration you never allow the needs of others to be too far from our hearts.

We, like they, are your people...and today we gather to pray for the future service of your servant and my father, Jeff Hood.

We know that we do not gather this day by happenstance and it is in this spirit of expectancy and destiny that we also recognize and join with all of the great cloud of witnesses who have gone before us to make this day possible.

Now, I lift Jeff up to you, Lord, that he, like Moses, might be your chief and your advocate amongst the people.

When injustice arises in Clayton County, make him an advocate for the least and grant him the necessary courage when the time comes to "Go and speak with Pharaoh..."

When it is time to lead in new directions, don't let him tarry...but rather grant him the fortitude and strength to follow manifestations and incarnations of your love and grace.

When he arrives at the water's edge and his enemies seem to be closing in, remind him, Lord, that you are the God who always makes a way out of no way.

When night comes and it is difficult to see, grant him the faith to never avert his eyes from the pillar of fire you have placed before him to always guide his path.

When those under his guidance stumble, grant him the power of speech and persuasion to turn those under his care away from the idols of worldly destruction towards paths of restoration and righteousness.

And finally, O Lord, when he arrives at the mountaintop and looks out, help him to recognize the land of promise, have the boldness to run toward it, the drive to cultivate all the riches he finds there, and the wisdom to never look back.

Grant us on this day and all that are to come the peace of simply knowing that our chief is your child.

In the name of the Father, the Son, and the Holy Spirit of God...

Amen.

20.

I had slowly been building up to this point. I would say that this was probably the sermon that best illustrates my transformation from a conservative evangelical preacher to a moderate evangelical preacher to a progressive Christian activist. Five days before I delivered this sermon, I stood outside the Georgia Diagnostic and Classification State Prison in Jackson, Georgia holding a sign begging our government not to murder or execute Troy Davis. The state didn't listen and the emotional weight of the experience was overwhelming. I knew that I would never be the same. Though I would preach far more progressive sermons...this rambling witness of a sermon launched my life as a prophetic activist. I talk about abortion as a way to neutralize the backlash...I regret this...because my views were and are far more nuanced than they appear to be here. Since I delivered this sermon, I have not been invited back to The Rock Baptist Church, the church were I grew up and the church that ordained me. Perhaps...once you go too far, you can never go home again.

The Rock Baptist Church

Sunday Worship

September 25, 2011

Would Jesus be a Christian?

I have entitled my message this morning: Would Jesus be a Christian? Or perhaps more fitting: Would Jesus be a Christian here in America? Or perhaps most fitting: Would Jesus be a member of this church? So often when we ponder what Jesus is like or what Jesus is...we project on to him our values, our lives, our politics, our morals, our ways of going about things. Ultimately, Jesus begins to start looking very similar to us. In John 10:10 (RSV) Jesus boldly states, "The thief comes only to steal and kill and destroy; I came that they may have life, and have it abundantly." This morning we are going to quickly journey through the life of Christ, largely in the book of John, using John 10:10 as our guide. John 10:10 serves as the key to unlocking the message of Jesus. John 10:10 is also the key to unlocking the questions of the hour: Would Jesus be a Christian? Would Jesus be sitting here in this church? Is Jesus in our midst?

Let's begin with the Lord's birth. Let's journey back to a night a long time ago... There were a couple of shepherds in a field relaxing with their feet propped up and perhaps drinking a few cokes. The heavens opened up. The shepherds were terrified and in cartoon fashion probably started running into each other. When the heavens broke open, the shepherds were scared. I can remember growing up, reading these stories, and being terrified at the thought of angels appearing to me. Brother Chip King, the former youth minister here at the Rock Baptist Church. used to tell us about terrifying things in other dimensions and I can remember many a night not wanting to hear anymore. Nevertheless, the shepherds were out in their field tending their sheep and the heavens opened up. The words of gold poured down from the sky, "Glory to God in the highest, and on earth peace, good will toward men" (Luke 2:14 KJV). The shepherds looked at each other in amazement and realized that they had a front row seat for the changing of the universe. The shepherds knew where to go. They were so excited that they started running. They arrived at an inn. They went out back. They saw this little hut. They asked about the whereabouts of the child and Mary...who is very much an independent kind of American woman...who greatly values her freedom and wants things her way...tells the shepherds I am so sorry the baby is not here...I decided to get an abortion. I decided to terminate the pregnancy. The child was incredibly inconvenient. These were highly irregular circumstances. I didn't think I would be able to get my education if I had the baby. I didn't think I would be able to do the things that I wanted to do in life...so I just decided to go ahead and have an abortion.

Now we all know that that's not the story, but what if it was. The Bible tells us that it is the thief comes to steal. Society tells many young women that if they have the child then a large amount of their life is going to be stolen from them. The Bible speaks differently though and often points out that...society is the thief. This idea of individualism and freedom that we have is the thief. The 'I' or 'me' based mentality is the thief. Jesus says, "The thief comes only to steal and kill and destroy; I came that they may have life, and have it abundantly" John 10:10 (RSV).

Growing up, I was very familiar with the constitution of the Rock Baptist Church. Each time a controversy came up, my memory of the bylaws and regulations were refreshed. Unfortunately, it seemed that I heard a particular portion of the Rock Baptist Church's constitution the most...the provision against drinking alcohol, playing cards, and dancing. I can remember many young ladies wanting to have a wedding reception with a toast involving champagne...no, no, no, not at the Rock Baptist Church. The constitution says no champagne, no toast. This church, dear friend, is an alcohol-free establishment. No father daughter dance. This church, dear friend, is a dance-free establishment. I heard about these provisions often, but, unfortunately, I didn't often hear a lot about Jesus in the church constitution. I know he is there, but, sometimes, I didn't hear about him as much as I would have liked to. What is the miracle we find in John 2? Jesus turns the water into wine. Join me in reading from John 2:1-11 (RSV).

On the third day there was a marriage at Cana in Galilee, and the mother of Jesus was there; Jesus also was invited to the marriage, with his disciples. When the wine gave out...

Now I don't know if any of you have been to a party lately, but when they start talking about the wine giving out...that means a considerable amount of wine has been drunk. That means they killed the wine. There were probably more than a handful of people intoxicated at this point.

When the wine gave out, the mother of Jesus said to him, "They have no wine."

What do you think that Jesus told her? Go on down to Moe's Package Store...

And Jesus said to her, "O woman, what have you to do with me? My hour has not yet come." His mother said to the servants, "Do whatever he tells you." Now six stone jars were standing there, for the Jewish rites of purification, each holding twenty or thirty gallons.

Now, let's first go with the small end of the numbers, twenty gallons times six jars. That is one hundred and twenty gallons of wine. Holy moly! They are getting ready to party.

Jesus said to them, "Fill the jars with water." And they filled them up to the brim. He said to them, "Now draw some out, and take it to the steward of the feast." So they took it. When the steward of the feast tasted the water now become wine, and did not know where it came from (though the servants who had drawn the water knew), the steward of the feast called the bridegroom and said to him, "Every man serves the good wine first; and when men have drunk freely, then the poor wine; but you have kept the good wine until now."

Translation, the headwaiter probably kicked his heels and shouted, "My, my, my, my where have y'all been hiding this tremendous wine!"

This, the first of his signs, Jesus did at Cana in Galilee, and manifested his glory; and his disciples believed in him.

Jesus provides one hundred and twenty gallons of the best wine and ya'll won't let people have a simple champagne toast? These people were getting excited and dancing. They were having the times of their lives and Jesus was right there with them. Jesus doesn't tell them to stop. Jesus tells them to fill up another cup. Jesus tells them to dance a little more. Jesus is the life of the party. Who are you, Rock Baptist Church, to demand otherwise? Jesus says, "The thief comes only to steal and kill and destroy; I came that they may have life, and have it abundantly" (John 10:10 RSV). Realize that abundance is not a quantity. It is not a moral code...what can or can't one do. Jesus says come to me. I am bringing the party. He didn't say stop. He said let's go.

I don't know if you know about this woman from Samar'ia in John 4:7-9 (RSV).

There came a woman of Samar'ia to draw water. Jesus said to her, "Give me a drink." For his disciples had gone away into the city to buy food. The Samaritan woman said to him, "How is it that you, a Jew, ask a drink of me, a woman of Samar'ia?"

Just recently, I saw a map of the United States showing where our evangelical brothers and sisters live. There are a considerable amount of black neighborhoods, white neighborhoods, Hispanic neighborhoods, Asian neighborhoods, and a whole host of other racially segregated neighborhoods...but not many multiracial neighborhoods. Evangelicals don't seem to be interested in living in multiracial neighborhoods. Jesus was interested in breaking down these types of divisions. Jesus showed up on the wrong side of the tracks. Jesus went into Samar'ia, asked for a drink, and ended up giving this woman of Samar'ia a drink of love that would restore her life forever. I know we have been talking about alcohol...but this was about the thirst of the soul for love and restoration. Jesus gave somebody, who one race despised and said was worthless, love and bound himself to her for all of eternity.

I am proud of you, Rock Baptist Church, for staying in this area when you could have ran. I know that it has not been easy at all. I am proud of you though, because I am finally starting to look out and see diversity. I can tell you that there was a time in the history of the Rock Baptist Church in which diversity was not valued. There are positive things happening here. We are starting to look at each other as human beings. We are starting to live fully in this a neighborhood and instead of moving out when things get difficult...we are locking down. That is the message of Jesus! That is the Gospel! I think about this neighborhood behind the church. I know the sign that sits there when you go into the neighborhood, 'Warning this is an area of gang activity.' You see the disciples were like many evangelicals out there... They were willing to go into many of the difficult subdivisions, but they preferred not to speak to anybody. They certainly didn't want to share a drink. They certainly didn't want to get to know anybody. But not you, Rock Baptist Church, you have gone back into the difficult neighborhoods and you are starting to have conversations. I am beginning to see diversity that is the result of being willing to talk to each other. Don't let it stop! Jesus says, "The thief comes only to steal and kill and destroy; I came that they may have life, and have it abundantly" (John 10:10 RSV). Do not dwell on racial differences...love each other! The thief wants you to go back to those old ways of racial hatred and bigotry. Keep growing into each other! Don't stop! Keep reaching out! Keep pressing in!

The Healing at Bethseda occurs in John 5:5-7 (RSV). Those who were sick would come sit by the pond. The angel of the Lord would come down and stir up the water every once in a while and the first one into the water got healed. So everyone who had an ailment was hanging out next to the pool, because when that water got to stirring up they wanted to be the first one in. Jesus walked up and...

One man was there, who had been ill for thirty-eight years. When Jesus saw him and knew that he had been lying there a long time, he said to him, "Do you want to be healed?" The sick man answered him, "Sir, I have no man to put me into the pool when the water is troubled, and while I am going...another steps down before me."

I ain't got nobody to just lift me up and toss me in the water. He has made it all the way to the pool, but he doesn't have anybody to pick him up and put him in. We have got a ton of people out there who are right on the edge of the pool and just need a little extra help to get in. We have got a lot of people who are trying hard...working four or five jobs. I saw a poor lady at Wal-Mart the other night who was so hunched over she could barely see the cash register...85 years old...working the 8am to 8pm shift...so that she could have health insurance. We have got a lot of people out there who are right next to the pool and just need someone to give them a little help and lift them in. We have got to think about these people. Jesus says, "The thief comes only to steal and kill and destroy; I came that they may have life, and have it abundantly" (John 10:10 RSV). The thief wants you to look at that person who needs just a little bit of help, who just needs a little lift into the pool and say I'm too busy. It's about me. I have got some things that I need to do. I have got things that I have to take care of. I don't have time to put you in the pool.

First, the enemy will take away our ability to run, then our ability to walk, then our ability to get up...but truth be told, many of the people who need our help were running just like you at one point. So often we think of ourselves as not being a part of the healthcare crises in our nation. I worked at a hospital this summer full of impoverished people in need of help. There were many nights I saw it...I was there...people who were sick being put out cause they couldn't pay no more. The insurance company had called and said we ain't going to reimburse you no more. I am not going to tell you the name of the hospital, it would be unfair to single one facility out for the sins of the system, but I will tell you that it has a large cross on the side of the building. I can tell you that the cross lighted up the skyline. I can tell you that the hospital was founded to be a Christian place for people who could not afford to go anywhere else, but there are these little green pieces of paper that have changed all of that. I wonder what Jesus is trying to tell us when he bends down and tells the man...

"Rise, take up your pallet, and walk."

Jesus reaches out, stoops down, and grabs hold of the man to say, "Rise, take up your pallet, and walk" (John 5:8 RSV). Brothers and Sisters there are a lot of people out there who need a hand to get up...not necessarily a hand out...but rather a hand to get up. I can tell you that at this hospital where I worked...we chaplains weren't always the bearers of good news. When things got tough and finances got tight, I was the one who got to go to the room and say, "I'm so sorry that you can't walk. I'm so sorry that you can't even hardly breath. Unfortunately, the doctor doesn't have time to come talk to you. We don't have the financial ability to keep you here and I am going to have to escort you out of the hospital." This doesn't sound like the ministry of Jesus to me. Jesus says, "The thief comes only to steal and kill and destroy; I came that they may have life, and have it abundantly" (John 10:10 RSV).

John 6:59-66 (RSV)...

This he said in the synagogue, as he taught at Caper'na-um.
Many of his disciples, when they heard it, said, "This is a hard saying; who can listen to it?" But Jesus, knowing in himself that his disciples murmured at it, said to them, "Do you take offense at this? Then what if you were to see the Son of man ascending where he was before? It is the spirit that gives life, the flesh is of no avail; the words that I have spoken to you are spirit and life. But there are some of you that do not believe." For Jesus knew from the first who those were that did not believe, and who it was that would betray him. And he said, "This is why I told you that no one can come to me unless it is granted him by the Father."
After this many of his disciples drew back and no longer went about with him. Jesus said to the twelve, "Do you also wish to go away?"

You see when the words got tough... Do you know what Jesus and the disciples consisted of before this moment? Often we think of 11 or 12...we think of a small band of men walking around with Jesus. No, we don't know how many there exactly were before this moment...but we know there was a lot. Can you imagine if there were tens of thousands? Tens of thousands of people following the Lord's every movement and he starts talking a little tough. Then they respond, "Oh no, no, no we can't go that far, we cant follow you anymore..." Wait a second, wait a second Brother Jeff...you are talking about my wallet. I can't go that far. Wait a second Brother Jeff you are talking about my freedom...my rights...my guns...I don't know if I can follow that anymore. Jesus then looked up and there was a small remnant that remained. The people looked straight at the Lord. Jesus looked at them and said, "Do you want to go too?"

This church has reached a time when those who are leaving have left. Those who are no longer going to support the ministry of this church in this community have left. Jesus is looking at all of you who remain and saying, "OK. Let's do this." There are hard times that will come. Brother James told us about some hard times this morning. You are in need of a little bit of money. There will be more hard times. I have heard about your air conditioners. I have heard them run actually. I know that there are times in which this church is in desperate need of money. If you have not heard anything else I have said this morning, I want you to hear this...those who stayed...those who remained...got the chance to walk with Jesus. Those who stayed got to see the miracles. Those who stayed got to see the Lord rise from the dead. Do you hear me? I can tell you that you will see greater things than these. Hold on to your pew. Hold on to your membership. Greater things are coming! Jesus says, "The thief comes only to steal and kill and destroy; I came that they may have life, and have it abundantly" (John 10:10 RSV).

John 8:1-6 (RSV)

...Jesus went to the Mount of Olives. Early in the morning he came again to the temple; all the people came to him, and he sat down and taught them. The scribes and the Pharisees brought a woman who had been caught in adultery, and placing her in the midst they said to him, "Teacher, this woman has been caught in the act of adultery. Now in the law Moses commanded us to stone such. What do you say about her?" This they said to test him, that they might have some charge to bring against him.

They said this to test him. Often times our friends and colleagues in the Christian world, especially here in the United States, will bring someone to us and they will say, "We've got em' now." We caught this woman in the very act of adultery. Jesus, you have been talking about grace and all of these flowery things. We have got you now. You have got to follow the Law of Moses. It looks like from the rest of the passage that Jesus said no to the Law of Moses and showed that he brought a new law. You know, Jesus has an incredibly clever wit about him. To show the new law, he stoops down and starts writing in the dirt. How many times have you seen the Christian community bring someone forward to be stoned? We have got him. We caught this one in the very act. Where is your grace now? The law says they must be stoned. Where is your grace now? Well...then and now Jesus stooped down and started writing. I tend to believe that Jesus stooped down next to the woman and started writing the names of the Pharisees' mistresses. How many times have you been the party who has brought the woman to be stoned? Often, we want grace but we are a little stingy with others. Why are we always so quick to execute and enact the punishment? If the Lord stooped down in front of you, what would he be writing in the dirt? Whose name would he pull out of your closet? What skeleton would he pull out and let it dance around?

When they wanted to kill her, Jesus said 'no'...Jesus says 'stop.' Jesus says 'my grace is higher than your law.' So often, I hear the catcalls for blood and retribution. Then, in the midst of the chaos, I hear a faint voice in the distance remind us that my way is higher...my grace is more powerful...my will is love. Jesus says, "The thief comes only to steal and kill and destroy; I came that they may have life, and have it abundantly" (John 10:10 RSV).

We live in a time of guns, violence, wars, and rumors of wars. How is the Christian community to respond? How is the Rock Baptist Church to respond? I did some fairly intensive emotional preparation for this sermon.

This past Wednesday night I found myself in Jackson, Georgia with my new wife Emily. I can tell you that I saw a considerable amount of hate in Jackson, Georgia. I saw hundreds and hundreds and hundreds of people, not only mourning the life of Officer Mark MacPhail, but also asking incredibly pertinent questions: Do we have to kill someone else? When will the cycle of violence stop? I went down to Jackson, Georgia to check out the situation involving Troy Davis for myself. You see, growing up at the Rock Baptist Church I was taught that life was something to be fought for. I was told to be pro-life. You told me that I needed to protect life at all costs. Your instructions got me down to Jackson, Georgia. I can tell you that the weight of those moments standing across the street from the penitentiary...from the death row chamber...were some of the weightiest moments I have ever felt. I saw a very diverse crowd crying out, "Please. Spare this man." I also saw the armies of the people lined up...the state patrol, multiple law enforcement agencies, state employees, and others...shouting, "Crucify him! Crucify him! Crucify Him!" As tears rolled down my face, I saw my tax dollars at work in front of me. I saw the armies of law enforcement telling me, "Back up! You are not a part of this. Back up!" I was standing next to a young man who looked up at me and said, "Our governor is a Christian...even more he claims to be a Southern Baptist...he claims to be an evangelical...Our President claims to be a Christian...All of these people who claim to be Christians have a chance to step in...and one by one by one they pass by...and I hear the calls to crucify Troy Davis grow louder." Make no mistake, I am not saying that this man was Jesus, but I do expect those who claim Jesus to act like Jesus.

I was holding up a sign at the protest begging for the life of Troy Davis to be spared. Then from my left, I briefly caught a glimpse of an older gentleman driving what looked to be a Cadillac Escalade. I am sure he is a member of one of the finer First

Baptist Churches in South Georgia. I saw this man turn into the crowd, a very angry man. It wasn't enough for this man to know that Troy Davis was going to be executed. He had to scream 'cop killer' out his window and turn his vehicle into the crowd. I saw the armies of Caesar aligned in front of me who had sworn to protect me. This gentleman hit me with his vehicle's side mirror. I was the one not paying enough attention to get out of the way. As he stopped and got out of his car...ready to rumble because someone messed up his car...I looked at his eyes to witness an unbelievable astonishing anger burning in his pupils. Not only did this gentleman want Troy Davis killed that night, he wanted me killed too. That slogan that everyone has been chanting, 'I AM Troy Davis,' took on new meaning for me as I saw the tires turn toward me. Jesus says, "The thief comes only to steal and kill and destroy; I came that they may have life, and have it abundantly" (John 10:10 RSV). It is the thief who steals. What are all Georgians this day after we took the life of Troy Davis?

Lazarus has fallen dead in John, chapter 11. The paid mourners are out there screaming and hollering...and Jesus says Lazarus is just sleeping. He is just asleep. Those who loved the Lord spoke saying, "If only you had arrived a little earlier, you could have stopped this." You know what Jesus says...he says, "Death doesn't have anymore power when I get here. You might threaten to execute me. You might actually execute me...but death doesn't have any more power when I show up."

John 18 and 19. We are getting closer and closer and closer to the time of execution. The Lord had appealed to the District Court, had appealed to the Governor, had appealed to his Congressman, he had brought people out to march, he had people really cutting up to try to save his life...and in the latter verses of John 18 we find Jesus standing before Pilate. Though his conscious was pricked, Pilate declared, "I am bound by the laws of this land and I am going to wash my hands to absolve myself of what you are about to do. I don't want any blood on my hands. It might mess up my nice rob and crown. I just don't want any blood on my hands."

I am going to go ahead and tell you something...until you get a little blood on your hands...until you get down in the mud with those who need our help and get a little dirty...the scriptures say that until you get down with the least of these you do not know Jesus. The Lord is telling us that he doesn't want us to just be sad when you see marginalization and oppression. Jesus says, 'I want you to feel it.' Jesus says, 'I want you to experience it.' Jesus says, 'I want you to get a little blood on your hands.' Rock Baptist Church is the place and is this the time where we are ready to get a little blood on our hands? Are we ready to go the next step and be the incarnation of Jesus Christ? You have done much from a distance...but I want to know if you are ready to get blood on your hands? Are you ready to get crucified with Christ? Are you ready to hang out with Jesus? Sometimes when we serve Jesus the executioner comes for us. Sometimes when we serve Jesus the executioner doesn't stop with Troy Davis...he comes knocking at your front door.

The people are aligned in front of Pilate. "Who do you want me to let go?" "Barrabas! Barrabas!" came the reply. "What do you want me to do with Jesus?" "Crucify him! Crucify him!" came the next reply. Let me tell you a little bit about Barrabas. We are told that the thief comes to steal, kill, and destroy. Barrabas had many of those bases covered...but it is interesting that we do too. When I think about destruction, I think about sitting at Jonesboro High School in Advanced Placement Statistics and seeing the World Trade Center towers crumble. I think about people jumping out of windows to avert the flames. In big red bold letters, President Bush vowed to catch Osama Bin Laden DEAD OR ALIVE. We wanted justice and retribution for what had happened. Barrabas was being held in prison due to the fact that he had fought the state. He had looked at the empire and been disgusted. He didn't want Roman domination. He didn't want Roman capitalism. He didn't want Roman influence. He didn't want Roman armies. He wanted to be free to be a Jew. So he rose up in opposition to the Roman Empire. He killed people to get his point across. He was for all intents and purposes a terrorist. He wasn't all that different from us as we make our ways through Iraq and Afghanistan. Barabbas was the worst that they could think of. Pilate did not want to crucify the Lord...so he put the worst he could find up there. The Jews said let Barabbas or Osama Bin Laden, go...we want to kill this man of peace. Whose side are we going to be on? Jesus says, "The thief comes only to steal and kill and destroy; I came that they may have life, and have it abundantly" (John 10:10 RSV).

In John 19, we find our Lord being beaten and crucified. Satan and all of his armies are watching in delight. They see Jesus hanging on the cross and know that they have won. They see the blood dripping from the hands. They see the blood dripping from the feet. I am sure that Satan declares a victory with a big wide grin. I wonder if he does not have the same reaction when we spend billions and trillions of dollars on national defense to kill people in foreign countries. I wonder if Satan doesn't have the same reaction. Satan grins as he creates confusion and people are dying. We are certainly playing into his hands with our thirst for more blood and revenge.

Jesus does not win when we go to war. Jesus is not winning in Iraq and Afghanistan. Satan is. Jesus says, "The thief comes only to steal and kill and destroy; I came that they may have life, and have it abundantly" (John 10:10 RSV). The thief is always the responsible party for death. The thief is always the responsible party for the bombs that drop. The thief is always the responsible party for the invasion of nations. In these activities the innocent die along with the guilty...

When the bombs drop they fall on the innocent and guilty alike. When the towers fall they fall on the innocent and guilty alike. Does this sound like Jesus or the thief to you? Does this sound like the Prince of Peace?

I don't know if you are aware of what happened on that cross many years ago...but Jesus did not hang alone. There were two other criminals hanging there too. On the crosses of Golgotha, the innocent died with the guilty. Before he died, the Lord said it is finished. The powers of the world unfurled their banners and claimed victory, "We have won."

I am sure there were many terrorists who saw the Twin Towers fall and thought they had won...but I am also sure there are many Americans who look to Afghanistan and Iraq to claim, "We have won." The Lord says to both parties, "Wait a second...you talk about justice...you talk about retribution...come, let me show you a higher way." You see if we look at the television and see people dying...then proclaim, "We have won." Who do we look like? Surprisingly, we don't look all that much different than Satan looked when he proclaimed victory after the events on Golgotha. Jesus says, "The thief comes only to steal and kill and destroy; I came that they may have life, and have it abundantly" (John 10:10 RSV). I don't know about you, but I don't want to cast my lot with the thief. I don't want to raise my fist to proclaim victory, justice, and retribution when people die. I want to cast my lot with Jesus who proclaims a higher way than death.

Christ has been crucified. The forces of evil have claimed victory. Friday was a very depressing day. Friday was the day for stealing, killing, and destroying. The story, however, does not end on Friday. On Sunday, the women...dare I say it again *the women*...come to the tomb to celebrate the life of Jesus in the midst of their grief. Then somebody pops up. Does this Jesus who arises go back to get revenge? Does he go and destroy the nations of the earth? Does Jesus go and destroy Pilate, Caiphas, and Herod? Does he seek any revenge against those who beat him and put him on the cross? The answer brothers and sisters is no. Jesus proclaims love. He proclaims love. Jesus lets the thief do the stealing, killing, and destroying. Jesus brings the abundance. Jesus says if you too will bind your heart to mine then you too will be known for love not hate. If you bind your heart to mine there will be no more need for blood to be shed. The follower of Jesus should know and believe that all the necessary blood has already been spilled. The price has already been paid.

Love is the answer now. No more need for violence. The price has already been paid. I am tired of the hypocrisy of our churches and leaders when it comes to violence and shed blood. Jesus says follow me...follow love. Jesus says, "The thief comes only to steal and kill and destroy; I came that they may have life, and have it abundantly" (John 10:10 RSV).

John 21:15-17 (RSV)

When they had finished breakfast, Jesus said to Simon Peter, "Simon, son of John, do you love me more than these?" He said to him, "Yes, Lord; you know that I love you." He said to him, "Feed my lambs." A second time he said to him, "Simon, son of John, do you love me?" He said to him, "Yes, Lord; you know that I love you." He said to him, "Tend my sheep." He said to him the third time, "Simon, son of John, do you love me?" Peter was grieved because he said to him the third time, "Do you love me?" And he said to him, "Lord, you know everything; you know that I love you." Jesus said to him, "Feed my sheep."

Peter was grieved due to the fact that he had previously denied Jesus. The weight of the moment got heavier with each question. John 21:19 (RSV):

And after this Jesus said to him, "Follow me."

We have arrived at the end of the Book of John together...and the Lord is asking us here this morning. Do you love me? Do you love me more than being right? Do you love me more than your political persuasion? Do you love me more than your wallet? Do you love me? If you love me...you will follow me. Sisters and brothers, I know that all the words I have spoken of this morning are tough. They challenge me. The way of Jesus is difficult...but the question Jesus asks of us is not whether it is difficult or not...the question he asks of us is, "Do you love me?" I know that this is a church that loves Jesus. I know that you are a people who loves Jesus. Will you lead the way? Will you lead the way? Will you show them love? Will you lead the way in fighting to end all stealing, killing, and destruction? The Rock Baptist Church should be a place where people can come and experience some moral clarity...the real Jesus. Not the Jesus who tends to look like us, loves who we love, and hates who we hate...but rather the real Jesus. The real Jesus says, "The thief comes only to steal and kill and destroy; I came that they may have life, and have it abundantly" (John 10:10 RSV). May we take this life-giving message to the world without end.

Let us pray

In the midst of the chaos of a violent world, let us be in peace and love God. In the midst of injustice, let us have the courage to say no and choose love. In the midst of state sponsored execution, let us have the courage to resist and choose love. In the midst of war, let us have the courage to not fight and choose love. In the midst of a healthcare system that is perpetually injust, may we have the courage to be healing and choose love. In all things, may our ears forever be open to the voice of the one who always chose love.

The benediction is simple...

Choose love.

Amen.

21.

I grew up in the Deep South. I had known injustice my entire life...but something happened on the day Troy Davis was executed at the Georgia Diagnostic and Classification State Prison in Jackson, Georgia. I could no longer accept injustice and seek to passively change it. I was now a nonviolent warrior for righteousness. My thoughts and sermons would not just be declared from pulpits...but rather would ordain signs and be shouted outside the many diverse institutions of oppression. Sometimes, I would be forced to fight against those I love in response to Jesus' incarnational vow to dwell with and become the least. This letter is a direct assault on the many privileged values and norms of southern universities and their football teams, I had once enjoyed.

Letter to the Editor of The Daily Mississippian

September 30, 2011

The Editor:

I experienced my first football game at Ole Miss not too long ago. Buying into the national advertising campaigns and recent attempts to modernize campus symbolism, I expected to see a modern multiracial environment. What I saw was quite the contrary...

I arrived in The Grove to see thousands of white people celebrating their money and football with exotic drinks, expensive clothing, and the finest tailgating tents money can buy. I stopped at my first tailgate to hear discussion of the joys of not being from Utah. To which a young man, donning a pledge pin from a large campus fraternity, replied, "...at least they don't have all these niggers." Honestly, looking around, I had no idea who he was talking about. The only persons on The Grove were members of Mississippi's white privileged elite. The Mississippians this young man seemed to be speaking of are unable to afford the tickets or comforts he and his buddies enjoyed. Somewhat shaken, I continued to journey toward the stadium. Upon gate arrival, I became more frustrated when I saw African-Americans filling most of the menial/servant tasks of cleanup and security. I bought a program from a vendor and wasn't surprised to see most of the players were also African-Americans. When I got to my seat, I noticed the crowd around me was all white. The longer I sat the more I realized where I was...the Roman Coliseum. Mississippi's white elites scream for blood as mostly young African-Americans place their lives on the line (see Bennie Abram) for collective white entertainment. I left knowing, despite trite cosmetic efforts to the contrary, the historical traditions of oppression are alive and well at Ole Miss.

The entire experience made me wonder when people will get as upset about inequality as they do loosing football games.

Rev. Jeff Hood

22.

Jesus said, "Greater love has no man than this, that a man lay down his life for his friends" John 15:13 (RSV). The people need the love of Jesus.

New Year's Day

Hood Family Worship

January 1, 2013

A Revolution of Hope and Love: A Sermonette

Get out of your comfortable cars, get out of your comfortable houses, and get out of your comfortable lives so that you can hear them. The people need the love of Jesus.

No one is an island. The longer that you seek to fortify your position on your island the more the darkness gathers and destruction rages. The people need the love of Jesus.

Today is the day to destroy your divided loyalties of race, tribe, class, and nation. The people need the love of Jesus.

It is time for you to weave a network of mutuality with this community so that you can join them in a single garment of destiny. The people need the love of Jesus.

Are you ready for their hopes and dreams to become your hopes and dreams? The people need the love of Jesus.

Will you fight against the forces of evil or give up? The people need the love of Jesus.

Are you ready to conquer your fears and serve Jesus? The people need the love of Jesus.

An impending revolution of hope and love is upon us.

Amen.

23.

My wife was pregnant with twins and I was tired. I began to preach in spurts. Often, the spurts just sounded like long slow cries for justice. Mississippi is a place that needs such cries...especially amongst its young evangelicals.

Tupelo, Mississippi

February 13, 2012

Brother, please make no mistake...God does not like segregated worship.

Tupelo, Mississippi

March 4, 2012

Jesus is with Rodney. If you are not with Rodney then you are not with Jesus.

Tupelo, Mississippi

March 11, 2012

We invite people into our home to live...because to not do so is to not let Jesus in.

Tupelo, Mississippi

March 25, 2012

If you would not rent your home to a black person then you are the problem with this society.

You cannot love a gay person and deny the very core of who they are. There is absolutely nothing loving about that.

24.

My wife did a presentation at an event called Summit at Abilene Christian University. After reading of their past and current treatment of queer folk, I decided to stand outside the chapel and hold a sign stating, "Jesus is Gay." I wasn't to the point where I knew enough to hold a "Jesus is Queer" sign...but I wanted to be counted on the side of justice. I wanted to make a stand and my voice was unquestionably heard. When I started conducting demonstrations like this and putting myself in danger...I began to realize that I was becoming the incarnation. I risked to love...

Abilene Christian University

October 9, 2012

Jesus is Gay

25.

I started work as a hospital chaplain at Huguley Memorial Medical Center and John Peter Smith Hospital. This experience exposed me to an entirely new way of preaching...one based on the traumas of life. The cries of justice grow stronger when someone is dying in front of you. This sermon provides questions as the answer to existential questions of meaning.

Huguley Memorial Medical Center

September 18, 2012

Who do you say that I am?

Mark 8:27-30 (RSV)

And Jesus went on with his disciples, to the villages of Caesare'a Philippi; and on the way he asked his disciples, "Who do men say that I am?" And they told him, "John the Baptist; and others say, Eli'jah; and others one of the prophets." And he asked them, "But who do you say that I am?" Peter answered him, "You are the Christ." And he charged them to tell no one about him.

The longer I seek to follow Jesus, the longer I seek to experience the incarnation of Jesus in this world, the more I realize that our faith rests on primary existential questions of meaning.

Who am I? Who do I see myself to be? Who is God? Who or what do I perceive God to be? Who are they? Who do I perceive the many people I encounter to be?

Modern Christians have often answered these questions using conservative typographies of faith that answer these basic questions thusly:

Who am I? I am someone in precarious and unmistakable trouble in constant desperate need of salvation.
Who is God? God is the angry man in the sky waiting to hurl down fierce loving judgment upon us...willing and eager to cast us into an eternal hell of our choosing.
Who are they? They are the ones more often than not destined to the fires of an eternal hell in need of our salvation. They are the ones usually outside of our club.

The problem with all of the aforementioned answers is that they are contrary to the incarnation-based and restoration-focused Gospel of Jesus Christ. We have to look to the love of God as expressed through Jesus Christ to answer these questions.

The former answers are evil answers because they lead us to evil conclusions. If we are evil persons in constant desperate need of an uncertain salvation then we are taught to hate the self and constantly be suspicious of the self. If we can't accept ourselves then how can we accept others? If we are constantly concentrating on the self and our sin, then how can we get to the heart of the other? This type of thinking pushes us to think of the self, other people, and God as other. Other is never us, it is always someone or something else. If we accept the previous answers then we never get to know our self, our God, and our neighbors here on earth. Why did Jesus come? Did Jesus come to send people to hell or did Jesus come that we might have life and have it in abundance? We must think about these things because they affect the very nature of how we interact with the self, God, and others. Jesus asks, Who do you say that I am?

Is the image of God existent in all people? When you enter a hospital room do you see the image of God lying there? When you encounter criminals is that somebody who is other? When you see Syrians dying in droves on television is that something distant? When you see our government killing innocent people with drones are those people who are other? Or is that you? Or what is more, is that Jesus Christ lying there? If we believe in a God who is up there, how are we to believe in a God within us and in them? If we believe that people of other faiths and beliefs are always going to hell, then how are we to recognize the God in them? The incarnational idea, that God is in us and in all people, changes everything.

I propose we change the way we formulate the root questions of identity.

Who am I? Genesis 1 says that you are the very image of God...the very image of the living God. When we believe that God is here and incarnated into this world...the question of God changes.

Who is God? God is here all around us. According to Matthew 25, God is the least of these among us. God is living on the street. God is thirsty. God is strange. God is in prison. God is on a respirator. God is here... God is represented in each and every human being. When God becomes something that is all around us, it dramatically changes the way we interact with the world. Issues of war, poverty, crime, oppression, economics...all of these things change because what we do to our neighbor or our self we recognize we are doing it to God. It is very difficult to kill, oppress, discriminate, steal from someone when you think that you are killing, oppressing, discriminating against, stealing from God. Who are they? God.

Sometimes the crosses, the paintings, the iconography, and the God talk distract from the fact that God has incarnated God's self into this world through God's son, Jesus Christ. The incarnation is the centerpiece of our faith. God became man so that man might become God. God is not up there. God is in you and in them. God is not other. God is always in you and all around. If you want to meet Jesus...maybe it is time to start loving your neighbor. The incarnation of Jesus is not just a past occurrence, it is a now occurrence and it is the only hope of humanity. May we meet the incarnation of God...in Jesus...as we meet our world. Jesus is asking us...Who do you say that I am?

Amen.

26.

I began to reformulate what I think God is. The love equivalency found in 1 John 4:8 revolutionized my life and the way I interact with God. No longer is God something abstract, but rather something I can touch, feel, and know...love. I founded a church with friends, based solely on this principle. This was our first sermon together.

The Church at The Hood House

December 2, 2012

LOVE

"He who does not love does not know God; for God is love."

1 John 4:8 (RSV)

In the book of 1 John we find one of the boldest proclamations in human history...God is love and love is God. What does such a statement mean? When we make love are we making God? This is a perplexing question in light of 1 John 4:8...but sex is not necessarily the primary focus of my talk this evening. The incarnation of Jesus illustrates what love is. Love is amongst us, knows us, and is willing to die to show us love. Love is always incarnational in precisely this manner.

We know this from experience. You always have to give something up and experience a momentary death of self in order to experience love. You have to risk. You can't be in a human relationship without a willingness to be incarnate and present with the other. You give in order to receive.

"Greater love has no man than this, that a man lay down his life for his friends."
John 15:13 (RSV)

Incarnation is always the key to understanding love. I am a follower of a love or God who incarnated herself into the world and ultimately gave himself so that others might live. In the crucifixion and resurrection we find the fullest manifestation of love. God/love incarnates into the world with the purpose of experiencing pain and dying so that others might live. The incarnation of God/love is the basis for any statement declaring God to be love...and if we are to be love incarnate in the world then we must be willing to be fully incarnate with the other and willing to die to love them. Such sacrifice is the outward expression of the inward presence of love.

Incarnation is always the key to understanding love. Divinity or love is always to be found here with us. The sacred always is incarnated into the secular to teach us the nature of the sacred. Love is not up there...it is here blossoming all around us. The incarnation means that love can always be found...even on the darkest of nights. The acts of love that we participate in are divine. The experience of loving someone else is divine. So where there exists love there too exists God, for God is love and love is God. When the words love and God become interchangeable then I think we will have captured what the writer of 1 John 4:8 intended to purvey.

Viewing God as love and love as God changes things. The secular becomes the sacred. God/love is always present amongst us in the acts of love/God that surround us. In the love we give and in the comfort of the arrival of the love we have longed for. The victory of God in this world is the victory of love in this world. We long for a world made right by love/God. So we join her in her fight to make the world right.

We like the God/love who incarnated love/God into the world...who lived and died so that all might love...die to our old selfish selves so that we might be resurrected in love. We have to give ourselves away. Everyone has the power to defeat the sin affliction that pushes us to not love...because since the beginning of time we have all had the image of God...the image of love implanted deep within us. In giving ourselves to others we break the sin affliction that so often holds us back. We must discover the love within us by loving the other. We cannot break free from our sin affliction of selfishness without giving our self to the world of the other. Love is incarnational.

In Matthew 25:34-36 and 40, the incarnate love/God says, "Come, O blessed of my Love, inherit the kingdom prepared for you from the foundation of the world; for I was hungry and you gave me food, I was thirsty and you gave me drink, I was a stranger and you welcomed me, I was naked and you clothed me, I was sick and you visited me, I was in prison and you came to me...As you did it to the least of these, the marginalized, the oppressed, you did it unto me."

Love is incarnational and the incarnate love/God tells us that the least, the marginalized, the oppressed is where you will find the greatest concentration of love. The world seems to love the least, the marginalized, the oppressed the least and thus God/love intercedes mightily on their behalf. If you want to know love then you must exist in the presence of God/the presence of love.

Tonight, I encourage you to find love in yourself, in others, and in the least. God is always present in the search for and creation of love.

"For love so loved the world that love gave love's only begotten love that whosoever believes in love will not perish but have everlasting life..." John 3:16.

Believe in God. Believe in love. Go make God. Go make love.

Amen.

27.

I continued to teach the basic principles of our faith...with the thought that love is what undergirds it all. Faith is the act of dreaming and wishing that God is present in the chaos.

The Church at The Hood House

December 9, 2012

FAITH

Faith is belief based on spiritual apprehension rather than tangible proof.

Faith is a matter of belief. Belief is a cognitive function. It is the mind declaring something to be, so often with minimal tangible proof in existential reality. Belief is a powerful tool...it propels people to leave the boundaries of what society deems possible or perhaps even real. By sheer belief persons have crossed oceans and space to discover new realities. Perhaps, this is what faith calls us to...belief that transcends the temporal boundaries of existential time and space to traverse the vast oceans and interstellar galaxies of our minds to arrive on the sores of new realities and dreams...even dare I say more real realities and dreamier dreams.

Faith is a matter of belief taking us beyond our existential borders to the vast land of possibility.

Faith is apprehensive. It is a burning desire for something beyond our existential reality to be true. We ignite the flame in our souls in hopes of what might happen or what might be true. Spirituality is the act of keeping this flame burning...to believe when all seems lost. It is the act of being alone in the world and believing that something or someone beyond this world loves us completely. It is the belief that the yearning deep within our minds and souls for that loving something or someone occurs not by accident...but rather to lead us to somewhere or someone. In the midst of a world that seems irreparably broken and often loveless, we cling to faith.

Faith is irrational. There is often no tangible proof for belief in the unknown, yet we cling to something. In the midst of death, many of us cling to a belief that death is not the end...that somehow someway death is not the final outcome. It is irrational to think that there is anything beyond this life...yet we believe. Faith is the expression of our often-irrational longings. Yet, perhaps it is in those irrational longings that we find that which is most human about us...hope.

Hebrews 11:1 (RSV) states plainly, "Now faith is the assurance of things hoped for, the conviction of things not seen."

Hope drives us to believe that the darkest nights do have a morning. Hope pushes us beyond ourselves to believe in a supernatural love that encompasses us all. In my life I am an unashamed peddler of hope. I believe when they can't think. I push when they can't walk. I carry when they can't stand. I love when they can't feel. I believe when they can't or won't. This is faith...forever injecting hope into the oppression that is human finitude or frailty.

Our irrational apprehensions push us to believe in hope. The hope that someone or something listens, the hope that someone or something will be waiting, the hope that someone or something loves, the hope that all is never lost...and so tonight let us hope together, let us learn to close our eyes to hope in that which we cannot see, let us set off from this place on a voyage of hope that will propel us to the shores of divinity that we might touch the dreamlike qualities of a God called love. Faith is the assurance of things hoped for.

Amen.

28.

I feel like our lives should consist of banging on the door of injustice. I have no doubt this is a point I have grown to. I have become a knocker.

Huguley Memorial Medical Center

January 10, 2013

Morning Worship

Luke 18:1-8 (NRSV)

Jesus "told them a parable about their need to pray always and not to lose heart. He said, 'In a certain city there was a judge who neither feared God nor had respect for people. In that city there was a widow who kept coming to him and saying, 'Grant me justice against my opponent.' For a while he refused; but later he said to himself, 'Though I have no fear of God and no respect for anyone, yet because this widow keeps bothering me, I will grant her justice, so that she may not wear me out by continually coming.' And the Lord said, 'Listen to what the unjust judge says. And will not God grant justice to his chosen ones who cry to him day and night? Will he delay long in helping them? I tell you, he will quickly grant justice to them. And yet, when the Son of Man comes, will he find faith on earth?'"

Often in this life we grow tired of fighting in the face of oppression. The sickness surrounds and chokes us. We, like the widow, plead for salvation and there seems to be no relief. When we look into our own souls, the oppressive sickness of the inner turmoil of the mind is consistently present. When we look to the lives of others, we find the oppression of the various physical sicknesses of life and the actions of others. When we look to our society, we find the sickness of a global society determined to oppress. It seems that no matter where we turn there exists the sickness of oppression. It seems that we are helplessly fighting a sick system of oppression that cannot be overcome. Take heart sisters and brothers, God spoke then and is speaking now.

We knock on the door of justice for ourselves. I am mentally ill. I have a sickness called bipolar disorder. The sickness is characterized by often-unpredictable cycles of mania and depression. I pray often that God would sustain me through the struggle of this disease. When things get the worst, I just keep beating on the door and pray that God will hear me. We all have our struggles, whether they are by our choosing or not, the question is... Are we going to remain persistent in prayer as we push through the struggles of life? In this parable, the afflictions of life are called injustice. Perhaps it is true that we are all suffering from some form of bipolar disorder, always perilously stuck somewhere between justice and injustice. Regardless of the condition, affliction, or the description, we, like the widow, must remain persistent in prayer in hopes that justice is coming and our minds will be restored to right. I believe that God is in the process of restoring all things...including you and me. We, like the widow, knock on the door of restoration.

We knock on the door for others. The patients that I visit in this hospital are sick. The friends and family members I minister to are sick. The random people I meet on the street are sick. Far too often we give up on those we come in contact with. Perhaps they talk too much or are too burdensome...but God does not give up on them and nor should we. I wonder if the widow would have received justice sooner if she had a multitude of people to join her. We pray and fight with those who need prayer and assistance...those longing for justice. I have found that when we fight for others we are also fighting for our selves. Jesus begged of the disciples in the Garden of Gethsemane... Will you stay awake with me? The widow is asking us the same question... Will you stay awake to knock with me? Will you believe that my standing in the community is as important as your standing in the community? Will you pray with me? The patients in this hospital is asking the same question...when all seems lost for them... Will you stay awake with me? Will you be the one who visits me? Will you pray for me? Don't grow tired. Be persistent like the widow in pursuit of justice. Prayer is an action and so we knock for others.

We knock on the door for our society. There seems to be little doubt that we aren't all that much different of a society than the widow existed in. We are surrounded by corrupted power. We are a society of injustice. We say that we want peace yet we continue to produce more weapons. We say that we want economic justice yet we consistently deny persons healthcare, food, shelter, and various other means of sustenance. We say that we care about the planet yet we continue to get bigger cars. When will we grow tired of the injustice?

There are billions of widows on this planet knocking at our doors and knocking on our hearts. For many, we are the judge...we are the oppressor. We are the ones who are denying entrance and justice. You work at a hospital that is part of a system that is denying quality healthcare to millions of people in our country and perhaps billions globally. Jesus said, "I am standing at the door and knocking..." God is with the widow. God is with those who our society consistently marginalizes. The question for us today is... Are we going to exist with the widow or the judge? Are we going to be with God or with man? Our prayers reflect the paths of our lives... Are you praying for justice? The widow is knocking on your door.

When the Son of Man comes, will he find faith on earth?

Let us knock. Let us pray.

Amen.

29.

For far too many years, I allowed myself to believe in the stone Jesus of the evangelicals. When I allowed Jesus to move...I got to see the greater things.

Huguley Memorial Medical Center

January 11, 2013

God of Stone?

Most days, when I pull into work here at Huguley Memorial Medical Center, I take a few seconds to look at the large monument of Jesus that sits on the front lawn of the hospital right next to the entrance. I can't stand that monument. I feel like it represents everything that is wrong with Christianity in the United States. The stone Jesus looks white, privileged, conservative, and powerful. I guess the stone Jesus is made in the image of those who funded it. This is unfortunate...as the real Jesus is much more eclectic, diverse, and exciting. Nevertheless, the stone Jesus can teach one major thing. Jesus moves.

The problem with the stone Jesus is that it can't move. I grew up worshipping the stone Jesus. I was always taught that God is the same yesterday, today, and forever. The problem with such thinking is that if you get it in your mind that Jesus is indiscriminately hurling lightening bolts of judgment and that Jesus is always going to be indiscriminately hurling lightening bolts of judgment. I was often taught that Jesus hated homosexuals, oppressed women, was suspicious of racial minorities, and was a rich white guy...and I thought that he always would be that Jesus. In the progress of life, I realized that sometimes we have to destroy the stone Jesus in order to reach the real Jesus...the Jesus who moves.

Jesus declared in Matthew 28:20 (RSV), "Lo, I am with you always, to the close of the age." Jesus is not stuck in stone. Jesus is moving with us. Jesus is experiencing our society as we are. Jesus moves in and with each age. In Matthew 25, Jesus said that he would always side with the least...the marginalized. The marginalized develops and changes and thus Jesus moves. I invite you to destroy your stone Jesuses so that you can move, change, and grow with the real Jesus.

Amen.

30.

This sermon explains everything that I now believe about God. I believe that God is incarnational. I believe that the incarnation of Jesus declares his abiding presence in the least, the oppressed, and the marginalized. I believe that Jesus is Queer. That is a long distance from where I started...but I have no doubt that God is here.

Huguley Memorial Medical Center

January 17, 2013

Jesus is Queer

I talk about Jesus today because I believe that Jesus is God made flesh. In 1 John 4:8 (RSV), John states unequivocally "God is Love." So Jesus is love made flesh. Love became flesh and dwelt among us. The love of Jesus is always incarnational. Jesus comes into the world to become that which he desires to save. In Matthew 25, Jesus also states that he will dwell most fully in the lives of the least, the marginalized, the oppressed. I love Jesus. I desire for the world to be restored to right.

I use the word "queer" as an all-encompassing word to describe lesbians, gays, transgendered, bisexual, pansexual, transsexual, and a whole host of related human sexual identities. The oppression faced by these groups I collectively refer to as queer is unmistakable. In many parts of our nation and world, queer persons wake up and wonder if they are going to make it through the day alive. There is a queer struggle for basic human rights in our country and around the world. Often the greatest source of oppression of queer persons comes from the faith that I belong to, Christianity. Instead of being a source of love and support, my faith is most often a source of oppression and violence. I speak today because I am a follower of Jesus Christ and I must.

I will engage the subject 'Jesus is Queer' in three main engagements.

First, we must respond to the subject 'Jesus is Queer' from a biblical perspective. Since God does not audibly tell us how to interpret the Bible each time we sit down with it...we must engage in the difficult task of interpretation. We, like generations before and after us, are entrusted with the difficult task of interpreting scripture. Those before us decided that the Bible justified slavery, genocide, the rape of women, infanticide, and a whole host of other evils. We reinterpret with love so as to not repeat the mistakes of previous generations. I am indebted to John Boswell's *Christianity, Social Tolerance, and Homosexuality*, Bruce L. Gerig's online essay "The Clobber Passages: Reexamined," Robin Scrogg's *The New Testament and Homosexuality*, and Rev. Jeff Miner and John Tyler Connoley's *The Children are Free: Reexamining the Biblical Evidence on Same-sex Relationships* for some of the content contained in the following formulation of my biblical perspective. Like these scholars, I do not believe the Bible condemns queer behavior and on the contrary encourages persons to not exchange their natural desires for unnatural desires. I speak so that we might choose the interpretation that is most consistent with the primary ethic of Jesus, love.

The first angry rebuttal I consistently hear when claiming that 'Jesus is Queer' is that Jesus cannot be involved or connected to something that the Bible considers sinful. This is a conclusion made based on six verses that directly mention queer sexual behavior out of over thirty one thousand one hundred verses contained in the Bible. These verses are inconclusive at best with regard to the conclusion that queer behavior is sinful. Most arguments first go to the story of Sodom and Gomorrah contained in Genesis 18 and 19. In the story, the men of Sodom attempt to gang rape two male-like angels who are visiting the home of Lot. To repel the men, Lot offered his daughters. The men declined and kept pushing for the two male-like angels. Ultimately, God destroyed the city for the wickedness there (and Gomorrah for similar evils). Nowhere in the text does anyone condemn queer behavior. The condemnation is that an evil inhospitable mob would try to gang rape complete strangers. The sex of the participants is not a concern for the men. These men were concerned with taking advantage of and humiliating whoever came into the town through gang rape. This was their horrible practice. The inhospitable wickedness of attempting to gang rape and abuse strangers is affirmed by Jesus in Matthew 10:12-

15 and Luke 10:8-12. Genesis 18 and 19 is about the brutal inhospitable sin of gang raping strangers.

In Leviticus 18:22 and 20:13 (RSV) there are what seems to be explicit mentions of queer behavior. 18:22 states: "You shall not lie with a male as with a woman; it is an abomination." 20:13 states: "If a man lies with a male as with a woman, both of them have committed an abomination; they shall be put to death, their blood is upon them." According to scholar Bruce Gerig, "The Hebrew word 'zakhar,' used in both passages to describe a male, is used ninety percent of the time elsewhere in the Old Testament to describe a man or male animal dedicated to a deity for a sacred function." Both of these passages seem to be about forbidding males to visit male prostitutes that are dedicated to pagan deities. Further evidence of this is found in Deuteronomy 23:17-18 which uses almost identical Hebrew words to describe prostitutes to pagan deities. We also are forced to wonder... If the inerrantists believe Leviticus 20:13 to be taken literally then why aren't they stoning queer folk? The truth of the matter is that in some places they are.

Before I close discussion of the Old Testament and queer behavior, I wanted to point out a few other possible instances of queer behavior. David and Jonathon enjoyed a relationship that seemed to leave the boundaries of a platonic friendship. In 1 Samuel 18:1-4 (RSV), we find a homoerotic encounter, "When *David* had finished speaking to Saul, the soul of Jonathan was knit to the soul of David, and Jonathan loved him as his own soul. And Saul took him that day, and would not let him return to his father's house. Then Jonathan made a covenant with David, because he loved him as his own soul. And Jonathan stripped himself of the robe that was upon him, and gave it to David, and his armor, and even his sword and his bow and his girdle." In 1 Samuel 20:30 (RSV), Saul angrily proclaims to Jonathon, "You son of a perverse, rebellious woman, do I not know that you have chosen the son of Jesse (David) to your own shame, and to the shame of your mother's nakedness? For as long as the son of Jesse lives upon the earth, neither you nor your kingdom shall be established."

According to biblical scholars Rev. Jeff Miner and Rev. John Tyler Connoley, in Hebrew culture, Saul's reference to shaming your mother's nakedness was generally understood to have a sexual connotation. In 2 Samuel 1:26 (RSV), David states unequivocally about Jonathan, "your love to me was wonderful, passing the love of women." It was not common then and it is not common now for heterosexual men to make such statements about each other. These verses combine to give fairly strong evidence that something more than a platonic friendship took place between David and Jonathan. Jesus is in the genetic line of David and was born in the City of David. In addition, also according to Rev. Jeff Miner and John Tyler Connoley, the same Hebrew word 'dabaq' that is used in Genesis 2:24 to describe how Adam felt about Eve is used in Ruth 1:14 to describe how Ruth felt about Naomi. The two loved each other intimately. I also wanted to quickly point out, with regard to

Leviticus 20:13, that there is not one example in the Old Testament's History of Israel of someone being tried and executed for queer behavior.

The Old Testament seems to celebrate queer behavior, not condemn it.

In the New Testament, there are also multiple passages of interest.

In 1 Corinthians 6:9-10, Paul lists types of persons who will not inherit the Kingdom of God. Some Bible translations translate two words in the passage as effeminate and homosexual and many others do not. The confusion is based around how to translate two Greek words 'malakoi' and 'arsenokoitai.' In Greek society, 'malakoi' was often associated with the youth who served as call boys. 'Arsenokoitai' is generally agreed to mean abusers of themselves with mankind. The disagreement comes with whether this word is referring to general queer behavior, those who are sexually immoral with boys, or specifically to male prostitutes in pagan temples. There were also numerous other Greek words available to Paul to better make his point if his point was to condemn queer behavior. According to Robin Scroggs, it seems much more reasonable that Paul was condemning call boys and prostitution rather than queer behavior.

In 1 Timothy 1:9-10, Paul gives a list of the types of men that the law is made for. In the list, Paul uses the Greek word 'arsenokoitai' again. In similar fashion to 1

Corinthians 6:9-10, the word 'arsenokoitai' could have multiple meanings...including referring to general queer behavior, those who are sexually immoral with boys, or specifically to male prostitutes in pagan temples. Many texts use the basic translation of 'those who defile themselves with mankind.' Since Paul refused to use the more explicit homoerotic words available to him, this passage also seems to be speaking of those who defiled themselves by being active with male temple prostitutes. This passage does not give a blanket condemnation of queer behavior. According to noted scholar John Boswell, no one in the early church connected the term 'arsenokoitai' with queer behavior until Hincmar of Reims in the 9th century.

The final major New Testament passage for discussion is Romans 1:26-27 (RSV), "For this reason God gave them up to dishonorable passions. Their women exchanged natural relations for unnatural, and the men likewise gave up natural relations with women and were consumed with passion for one another, men committing shameless acts with men and receiving in their own persons the due penalty for their error." Although there is language that can be disputed in this passage, there seems to be little reason to discuss it...as this passage is primarily speaking to heterosexuals. This passage has nothing to do with queer persons...as they would remain unchanged. This passage seems to have much to do with the danger of rejecting God. Paul directly states that it is evil for someone to exchange that which is natural for that which is unnatural. I take this as an endorsement of letting sexuality develop as it should naturally. There is a warning in this passage about trying to change queer folk. Paul understood that that which is natural is preferable to that which is unnatural. According to the Norwegian Natural History Museum of the University of Oslo, apart from humans, there is documentation that over 1,500 other species that exhibit queer behavior. That which is natural...

According to biblical scholars Rev. Jeff Miner and John Tyler Connoley, queer behavior is cited in multiple other New Testament passages. In Matthew 19:12 (RSV) Jesus refers to "eunuchs who have been so from birth." In the ancient world the phrase "born eunuch" often referred to queer men. In Matthew 8:5-13 and Luke 7:1-10 the Greek word 'pais' is used to describe the servant of the Roman centurion who Jesus heals. This word was often used in Greek to refer to a younger same-gender partner. In Acts 8:26-40 the Ethiopian is described as a eunuch. This was again the word often used to refer to a man who was queer.

Despite the fact that queer behavior was common in his era, Jesus never once explicitly forbade queer behavior. I believe this to be the strongest evidence in the Bible of the acceptability of queer behavior. Paul and others' failure to explicitly use words to describe queer behavior that were common in their time...provides evidence to the fact that Paul nor any other New Testament writer ever explicitly condemned queer behavior. If queer behavior was such an important issue then why is the New Testament not clearer on the issue?

The Bible is always an important tool for guidance in the lives of followers of Jesus…but let us not forget that the Bible is not God. In every generation, we have to choose to value either Jesus' love commandment in Mark 12:31 (RSV) to "Love your neighbor as your self" or to continue using the Bible to justify our prejudices and oppressions. We are at such a point in history. The Bible will be used, based on controversial interpretations, to say that queer behavior is a sin, but I hope that you are able to walk away from this talk realizing that the evidence for the 'queer behavior is sin' translation is at best highly controversial and at worst a result of the queer phobia of the translators. In light of Jesus' command in Mark 12:31, the best Biblical way forward is to start loving your queer neighbor as your self. Would you want someone to assault you for kissing your wife or husband in public? Would you want someone to call you and your wife or husband holding hands disgusting and revolting? Can you imagine the government saying you cannot get married, the church saying you are not a Christian, the school saying you are prone to molest children, the church saying you cannot be a minister, or a whole host of other wrongs? Christians must stop being known for the oppression, discrimination, assault, and the overall abuse of queer folk. Jesus said in John 13:35 (RSV), "By this all men will know that you are my disciples, if you have love for one another…" May we wake up to the words of Jesus in scripture and become known for love.

Second, we must respond to the spirit and events of our age. We do not live in a vacuum. If we are to live out Jesus' commandment of Mark 12:31 (RSV) to "love our neighbor as our self" then we cannot be silent in the midst of injustice. Hate crimes are notoriously difficult to document. Often victims of violence in less progressive regions and sometimes in more progressive regions are documented like any other victim. Sometimes victims are frightened to reveal all of the details of a crime out of fear of further retribution. I say all of this to point out that, while shocking, these statistics are likely higher than what is given. In 2011, according to The National Coalition of Anti-Violence Programs, 30 people were murdered as a result of their queer sexual identification. In 2011, according to the FBI, there were over 1300 hate crimes committed against queer persons. If you think these are crimes taking place far away from North Texas...last November 30, Carrollton, Texas police discovered the brutally beaten and mutilated body of actor Dustin Reeb and arrested Nathanael Greer who admitted that he killed Reeb due to his sexual orientation. Reeb was a committed Christian and active member of the Metropolitan Community Church of Greater Dallas. This was one of our brothers and most churches have let out nothing more than a whimper over this incident.

Hate crimes, however, do not tell the whole story. Each year, according to Suicide Prevention Education Awareness for Kids, it is conservatively estimated that over 1,500 queer youth commit suicide. When adults are included in such a count, the numbers are much higher. Just in the last six months in my time as a chaplain at

John Peter Smith Hospital and Huguley Memorial Medical Center, I have encountered 15 different families dealing with the attempted or actualized suicide of a queer person. Ten of these were 25 years of age or younger. Of these ten, eight victims or families described the oppression of conservative Christians as a prime reason for their attempted or actualized suicide. For these young persons…we are certainly doing something very wrong. In light of these alarming statistics, we must ask our selves: Are we are going to stand on the side of love or hate? Are you responsible for the promotion of hate? Are you responsible for stifling the love of Jesus with your own prejudices? Are you on the side of love or hate? I know who Jesus stands with…

Third, we must realize that we serve a God who is incarnational. Our God came down from heaven and became man so that God might dwell amongst us. Our God has experienced our pain and knows the human experience intimately. The injustices of this world were the reason that God came to earth in the form of Jesus. Through the incarnation, God is making all things right. The incarnation is the highest example of love. It is the physical representation of God's desire to dwell with us.

Jesus Christ came to experience the injustices of this world so that he might save us from the injustices of this world. God in the form of Jesus became what he wanted to save. Jesus sets an example that a love that saves is always incarnational. God is always going to those that we marginalize and oppress. Jesus declares quite plainly in Matthew 25:40 (RSV): "...as you did it to one of the least of these my brethren, you did it to me." Jesus exists in the lives of the least. God exalts and becomes the marginalized to save the whole. The least, the marginalized, the oppressed are always exalted to the point where they actually become Jesus through the experience of marginalization and oppression.

Our oppressions and marginalization have made queer folk one of the most marginalized and oppressed groups in our society...but thank God we have the miracle of the incarnation of Jesus to liberate all of our hearts, minds, and souls. Jesus incarnates himself into the lives of the queer community to save not only them but us too. I have not doubt that Jesus is presently with the queer community in their struggle for equality and basic human rights.

I have not doubt that the churches that do not stand with the queer community are not standing with Jesus. To know Jesus is to know those whom he says he will dwell in. Right now, it seems that Christians, just like the Pharisees of old, are leading the charge when it comes to the oppression of Jesus. We are kicking him out of our churches and pulpits for the idolatry of prejudice. We are forbidding our children to go near him for the false God of prejudice. We are the ones holding the stones of oppression. We are the ones who love our lofty prayers and music but hate our sisters and brothers. Today, you must ask yourself... Do you love Jesus more than your prejudices? In a society so often hopelessly devoid of love and justice, I know where I will stand…with the God who is love and queer.

Jesus is Queer…and if you want to be a follower of his then you need to find a way to become queer too…

Amen.

31.

I felt like this would be a good piece to conclude this collection. I wrote this blog as a biographical piece to tell of my encounter with the Queer Jesus. It represents the very best of who I am and whose I am.

Believe Out Loud

http://www.believeoutloud.com/latest/queer-jesus-saved-my-soul

March 1, 2013

Before my feet could touch the ground under the pew of the Southern Baptist church of my youth, I was afraid. Every time the preacher screamed and pointed eternal damnations, I knew he was screaming and pointing at me. Sunday nights were awful. The fears were fresh and pressed deeply into the soft tissue of my heart. As sleep was elusive, I prayed and wept throughout the night.

There was no answer. There was no salvation. I was only a child.

The Wednesday nights of youth worship and festivity were anything but fun. We were being trained. We were expected to be the warriors that would win the nation back for the Jesus Christ of the Southern Baptists. These battles began in our own group. I remember Sam. A regular attendee of youth services, Sam let it slip one night that she thought another girl in the group was cute. The total alienation of Sam commenced. I didn't stop it. I was too afraid.

Not too long afterward, Desmond shot himself. My childhood best friend was dead. When I was told that he struggled with his sexuality, based on the Southern Baptist theology I was taught, I assumed he was being punished. God was punishing Desmond for being attracted to other boys and killed him. When I realized I found another boy at school handsome, I knew I was next. Based on the teachings of my Southern Baptist church, I knew I was disgusting. I thought about suicide. I begged. I feared. There was no answer.

Southern Baptist elders teach young persons to feign certainty from an early age. The advice might translate into, 'scream until you can't hear the doubts anymore.' I had many doubts, so I screamed. I met Becky in my chemistry class in high school. One day, Becky told me in confidence that she was a lesbian. Though I was often uncertain if I even believed in God, I told her and everybody else in the class that she was going to hell. When others in the class confronted me about my behavior, I knew I was being persecuted for the Kingdom of God. The hateful screams toward Becky solved my lack of faith temporarily.

I spoke out of my fear. I chose not to love.

When I was asked to give a talk to a youth group, I spoke about the favorite topic of Southern Baptist culture warriors: homosexuality. I delivered an impassioned loud scriptural rebuke of a homosexual lifestyle. I spoke harshly. Although I questioned the harshness of what I was saying, I knew that I had to keep saying it if I wanted any level of certainty in my walk with Jesus. I was a fearful Southern Baptist homophobe.

Privileged friends and beautiful people are difficult to turn down, so I joined a fraternity. For obvious reasons, most of my friends were drawn to a way of talking about God called Calvinism. The base line of Calvinistic thought is that God has elected persons to be Christians. In many conservative spaces, the election of God also extends to those granted power and privilege. I liked this system, as it provided the answers and space for upward social mobility I hungered for.

I squashed my doubts with answers and the enjoyment of privileged posh spaces. In this space, no one claimed an alternative sexual identity and we honestly didn't think any existed, at least within the state limits. I was a culture warrior, with a bright shiny new academic theology, willing to engage in tremendous oppression. I was a privileged Southern Baptist Calvinist.

Those of us from the South know that sometimes it takes leaving for a little while to realize the ignorance of the land that we love.

I left. I accompanied my newfound peculiar Southern Baptist mentor, George, to a major northern city. There, I witnessed the unbelievable poverty and violence of an urban center, the vibrancies of a community called alternative, overwhelming diversity, and the power of the church to help and hurt in such settings. I concocted a plan to keep my privileged theology, while also helping people in the city. I wanted to have my cake and eat it too.

When the time came to choose a seminary, I had not doubt where I would go, the Harvard of Southern Baptist education, the Southern Baptist Theological Seminary. I was a privileged Southern Baptist Calvinist with a newfound festering miniscule social conscience.

Sweat poured, my chest pounded, my brain throbbed, my spirit was stifled, and my voice was weak.

I had spent a semester and a half at the Southern Baptist Theological Seminary and realized that the answers were running out. The professors consistently argued that those who cut out one piece of Calvinistic theology or the Bible, would begin the downgrade that led straight to hell. I knew that I was on the downgrade and I was flipping out. I felt like I was going to be eternal toast. I started asking questions and things got much worse. 'A Christian wouldn't ask such questions.' 'You must not be saved.' 'Those who doubt are on the downgrade.' 'If you can't believe then maybe you aren't chosen.' All of these responses served to push me toward suicide.

I turned to my peculiar Southern Baptist mentor, George, for help. "I am dying," he said. I didn't believe in God or much of anything anymore, but I believed in George. Though I was frightened, I stayed awake with him. As his time on earth drew to a close, George asked me to come into his room alone, he grabbed my hand, pulled me close enough to smell the death, and told me, "I am gay and always have been...Go back to seminary and fight for those who have no voice." I didn't believe. I was confused. This was the beginning.

The events of life demanded answers that the Southern Baptist Calvinists didn't have.

I pushed. They screamed louder. I questioned. They demanded silence. I hurt. They ignored. I cried out to a God I didn't believe in to deliver me. I was alone. I needed help. As I shared my story, several Southern Baptists came out to me. They knew I was safe. I rediscovered hope. I began to believe again. I began to discover the Queer God. After graduating, I retreated to Emory University's Candler School of Theology. I thought the mainline folks I met there would accept me. They didn't. There was much suspicion around my zealous desire to question their theology too.

I served on a panel about LGBT issues. I was called conservative. I didn't know any better yet. One person on that panel began to meet with me and love me, Duncan. The regal gentleness I discovered in him changed me.

Later, I met Lucas, an activist, who also loved me and challenged me to go deeper still. These two men prepared my soul to meet the Queer Jesus. I finally found love and acceptance in a community I previously called 'sin.'

On the way down to Abilene Christian University to hear my wife speak, I began to read of the many atrocities committed against Queer folk by faculty and students of the institution. I knew that following Jesus means action. I knew that my faith would no longer allow me to exist in these bigoted spaces without acting.

I drew up a sign declaring, "Jesus is Gay." In the midst of my naked fear, as insults flew on the steps of the Chapel, I experienced Jesus. I became Queer.

I cannot stop talking about this being I have met. I protest. I write. I speak. I preach. I fight. I love. I hope. I have a testimony of a Queer Jesus who, through the folk called Queer, made me whole through discovery of my own Queerness.
I know it is the churches and people called 'Christian' that need the Queer Jesus the most. These are my people, and thus, I work. I work so that my two sons, Jeff and Phillip, might know a church where Jesus is not shunned for Queerness either.

Sources:

Bruce L. Gerig. "The Clobber Passages: Reexamined." Retrieved from http://epistle.us/hbarticles/clobber1.html and http://epistle.us/hbarticles/clobber2.html on 14 December 2012.

John Boswell. Christianity, Social Tolerance, and Homosexuality. Chicago, Illinois: University of Chicago Press, 1980.

Robin Scroggs. The New Testament and Homosexuality. Minneapolis, Minnesota: Augsburg Fortress Press, 1984.

Jeff Miner and John Tyler Connoley. The Children are Free: Reexamining the Biblical Evidence on Same-sex Relationships. Indianapolis, Indiana: LifeJourney Press, 2011.

Lila Shapiro. "Highest Number of Anti-Gay Murders Ever Reported in 2011: The National Coalition of Anti-Violence Programs." The Huffington Post. Retrieved from http://www.huffingtonpost.com/2012/06/02/anti-gay-hate-crimes-murders-national-coalition-of-anti-violence-programs_n_1564885.html on January 14, 2013.

Mary L. Bonauto and Jeffrey Robbins. "Rising Hostility against LGBT Americans belie gains." The Boston Globe. Retrieved from http://www.bostonglobe.com/opinion/2013/01/15/podium-lgbt/RWUuvnDT4Ldvjodf0HNFAP/story.html on January 16, 2013.

News Medical. "1,500 Animal Species Practice Homosexuality." The Norwegian Natural History Museum of the University of Oslo. Retrieved from http://www.news-medical.net/news/2006/10/23/20718.aspx on January 16, 2013.

Steven Sprinkle. "Suspect in Gay Murder Arrested in North Texas Homicide; Confesses to the Crime." Unfinished Lives Blog. Retrieved from http://unfinishedlivesblog.com on January 15, 2013.

Suicide Prevention Education Awareness for Kids. "Suicide Facts." Retrieved from http://www.speakforthem.org/facts.html on January 14, 2013.

Afterward

"A man there was, though some did count him mad, the more he cast away the more he had."

— John Bunyan, *The Pilgrim's Progress*

Jeff Hood and his seventeenth century Baptist, Non-Conformist forebear, John Bunyan, share much in common. Like Bunyan, Hood is no docile soul. He has seen things as they are in the world of faith, and asked, "Why?" Moreover, like Bunyan, Hood has chosen to do something about it.

What Hood has produced here is a spiritual autobiography, but it is more than that. Like the wayfarers at the Inn of Gaius in *The Pilgrim's Progress*, Hood cracks the hard shell of evangelical orthodoxy to break open the meaning of the riddle of the Gospel: One gets by giving away all that one has—one is born by dying—one finds one's way by going on pilgrimage into the Unknown. Bunyan wrestled with spiritual and social injustice in the England of his day, and it earned him misunderstanding, enmity, opposition, and at least two lengthy jail terms. Without his long seasons of spiritual turmoil, however, he could never have produced *The Pilgrim's Progress.* Likewise, Hood's account of spiritual turbulence, culminating with his saving encounter with the Queer Christ, has enabled him to give us this important chronicle of a refreshed and queered preacher/activist on a spiritual pilgrimage—a prologue, perhaps, to a radical evangelical *Progress* for the twenty-first century.

Hood writes with brisk candor and hard-won common sense about the way forward for evangelical Christianity. Either its fortress mentality will continue to sequester itself from the hopes and dreams of the young, or it will strike out with them and with non-conformist preacher/activists like Hood to discover a new face of God among the dispossessed, the outcasts, the ignored, and the poor—in other words, the "queer" of this age and of the age to come. Old wineskins will not bear the heady ferment of the new wine. New wine must be poured into fresh wineskins (Mark 2:22).

What is offered in this book is a boldly Christocentric, Christ-like journal of spiritual transformation. There is no allegory here, no riddle, no veiled meaning. Instead, Hood offers his readers a challenge as clear as the Invitation to Christian Discipleship offered at the conclusion of a Baptist sermon: Decide!

At the conclusion of Part Two of the *Progress*, Bunyan speaks across the years through the voice of his character, Valiant-For-Truth: "My sword I give to him that shall succeed me in my pilgrimage; and my courage and skill to him that can get it." Jeff Hood, I believe, has heard that call, and picked up Bunyan's bright sword, transforming it into a queer pilgrim's staff for the journeys of faith and hope stretching out before himself and us. There is nothing "mad" about him, or angry either. He simply understands that the more unnecessary baggage one leaves behind, the more swiftly one progresses along The Way.

Stephen V. Sprinkle, Ph.D.

Professor of Practical Theology, Director of Field Education and Supervised
Ministry, and Director of Baptist Church Studies
Brite Divinity School
Fort Worth, Texas

Theologian-in-Residence at Cathedral of Hope
Dallas, Texas

Now

Poet, Pastor, Activist and Writer

Sermons and Writings

revjeffhood.com

The Church at Mable Peabody's

https://www.facebook.com/TheChurchAtMablePeabodys

knowing that love is the queerest of all constructs. go now and be queer. amen.